I0089430

AUTISM QUESTIONS TEACHERS ASK

& THE ANSWERS THEY SEEK

AUTISM HELP SERIES
BOOK TWO

DR. SHARON A. MITCHELL

ALSO BY DR. SHARON A. MITCHELL

Autism Series

Autism Goes to School

Autism Runs Away

Autism Belongs

Autism Talks and Talks

Autism Grows Up

Autism Goes to College - Jeff's Coming of Age Story

Autism Box Set (the first 5 books in the series)

Autism Questions Parents Ask & Answers They Seek

Autism Questions Teachers Ask & Answers They Seek

Anything for Her Son (free short story - download at https://dl.bookfunnel.com/a27d9uzou0)

Psychological Thrillers

GONE

TRUST

SELFISH

INSTINCT

REASONS WHY

MINE

SANCTUM

WHEN BAD THINGS HAPPEN BOX SET

Farmers of Goodrich County Romances

(Clean & Wholesome Romances + autistic characters)

Copyright © 2023 by Dr. Sharon A. Mitchell

All rights reserved.

Print ISBN: 978-1-998111-03-9

No part of this book may be reproduced in any form or by any electronic or mechanical means, including information storage and retrieval systems, without written permission from the author, except for the use of brief quotations in a book review.

CONTENTS

WHEN BAD THINGS HAPPEN SERIES

GONE: A PSYCHOLOGICAL THRILLER PREVIEW

FOREWORD

When you entered the teaching profession, your goal was to make a difference in the lives of children. And, you are.

What they likely didn't tell you about during those years of teacher training was the vast diversity of the students who would find their way into your classroom. In particular, you probably had little training about autism.

You have just learned that an autistic student will be entering your room. Don't panic! With a bit of help, you've got this.

Teachers are busy people. In fact, the reason why I wrote five novels about autism was because I heard over and over from parents and teachers that they were pushed for time, often hanging on by their nails, and didn't have spare hours to study textbooks or wade through internet sites. So, I wrote about autism in an easy-to-read style, telling stories about autistic kids, their families and teachers and how they implemented strategies.

Outsiders don't get it about teaching. Yes, your actual amount of student contact hours during a week is fewer than the average office worker puts in. But those five or six hours a day do not at all reflect the amount of time and effort that teaching requires. Even when you're not marking or planning, chances are your students are foremost in your mind and you are constantly thinking about ways to teach. In addition to that, you do have a life outside of school.

As a professional who doesn't have a lot of free time, this book was written with you in mind. There is no need to start at the beginning and read the whole book through (although you can if you want to). Instead, browse the table of contents and jump to the chapters that might apply to the question that is in your mind right now.

Throughout the book there are links to further illustrate points or if you want to dive deeper into the subject. Since some of you prefer to learn by reading and others by watching or listening, some of the links lead to articles while others will take you to videos or audio recordings.

I understand that you are just one adult, trying to serve the needs of so many students in your class. Although this book focuses on autism, the strategies you'll find here will apply to many of the diverse learners within your room.

Although about four times more boys are diagnosed with autism than girls, it is debated that our current tests miss some of the symptoms in girls. But, to avoid that dreaded he/she in this book, I'll refer to a generic he, keeping in mind that this applies to girls as well.

Autism is a difference - a different way of viewing and responding to the world. Once you get a glimpse of how this world might feel for an autistic student, then inclusion becomes easier and more productive.

The literature on resilience talks about how just one adult who takes the time to get to know a student to understand and encourage him, can make all the difference in that child's life. YOU can be that adult for your autistic student this year. This book will help. (You might also want to share with parents the companion book *Autism Questions Parents Ask*[1]).

What follows is a compilation of questions I have often been asked. I'm a former teacher, psychologist, school consultant, autism consultant and a parent. I can help you look at autism for all these views.

At the end of the book there is a Reference section with links to further information for each chapter.

Sigh.

The internet being what it is, things change. Rapidly. While at the time of printing, the links are all accurate, that could not be true two years from now, or even tomorrow.

If a link you're interested in does not seem to be working, try typing the url into TheWayBackMachine at https://archive.org/web/.

You might also be interested in this book for parents:

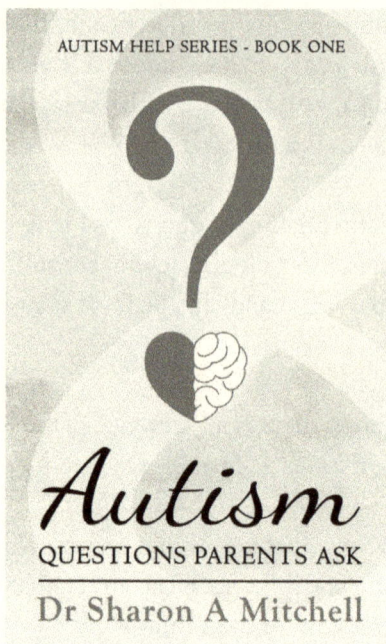

AUTISM HELP SERIES - BOOK ONE

Autism

QUESTIONS PARENTS ASK

Dr Sharon A Mitchell

[1] Https://Books2Read.com/AutismQuestionsParentsAsk.

WHAT IS AUTISM ANYWAY?

A utism is a spectrum disorder. That means that there is a large variation in how the autistic symptoms play out in individuals. For some, it seems that the autism characteristics permeate every moment of their day. For others, these characteristics can appear more muted. But within one person, functioning can vary throughout different life stages, or even throughout the day.

Autism has a genetic basis, and this is the way the child comes. Some parents say that they could tell from birth that there was something different about the way their infant related to the world. With other children, the differences aren't as apparent until the preschool years. (If you're interested in the neurobiological basis of autism, take a look at the chapter What Caused Him to Have Autism). Autism is not a result of any parenting style.

An autistic student has challenges in social communication. That could range from being unable to speak, to coming across as socially awkward. Even in those who are highly verbal, there will be difficulties with communication, especially in the nonverbal realms. Challenges in reading body language and understanding subtleties and subtexts make socializing difficult. We'll talk more about the language difficulties in the chapters:

- What If He Can't Talk?
- Why Does He Speak Sometimes but Not At Others?
- Auditory Sensitivities.

There will be repetitive interests and/or behaviors, although each of these can change over time when some other topic or action becomes the focus. We'll discuss some of these repetitive actions in the chapter on stimming.

Along with behaviors go what are sometimes referred to as restricted interests, although I'm not a fan of the word "restricted" in this case. In many kids, it comes more as an intense interest that consumes their attention for time spans that are far longer than demonstrated by their peers. There are some clear advantages to having restricted interests. Your student may know far more about his area of interest than anyone you've ever met. If this interest can one day be translated into a job, it's a win-win. Monotropism is a feature of autism. Monotropic minds focus their attention on a narrow but intense number of interests, often overlooking things that are not within this tunnel of interests. This is sometimes referred to as stimulus over-selectivity.

Dr. Damian Milton describes monotropism as getting into a flow state where your attention is fully taken up with the activity itself. Being in that flow state can help reduce stress and result in learning. Through entering a flow state, an autistic student can gain control over his environment, an environment that can easily assault his sensory system. Listen to what Dr. Milton[1], (who is autistic himself) says about monotropism and having an autistic child in your classroom.

Fergus Murray is a science teacher and an autist (autistic person). He's written a nice article, Me and Monotropism: A Unified Theory of Autism[2].

It is a rare autistic student who is not bothered by sensory sensitivities in one or more areas. His body can be under-responsive, requiring more input before the sensations register or over-responsive where even slight bits of stimuli are bothersome at best, if not painful. In fact, sensory issues play such a significant role in an autistic person's life, that we're devoting nine chapters of this book to this topic, beginning with What Is It with This Sensory Stuff?

When you put together communication issues, difficulty with socialization and sensory sensitivities, you might understand how autistic kids might be anxious. Anxiety is not part of the diagnostic criteria for autism, but it is a common co-existing condition.

Other mental health conditions, such as mood disorders can also co-exist with an autism diagnosis. In addition, some autistic kids will also have an intellectual disability. It is debatable just what proportion of autism people are also intellectually disabled. We'll talk about this more in the chapter Is He High or Low Functioning?

One of the best explanations of what autism is comes from Sara Harvey in her talk, What Is Autism to You? [3]She speaks of what she knows - both she and her daughter are autistic.

~

When a diagnostician is assessing if a child might be autistic, the following criteria are considered:

1. Persistent deficits in social communication and social interaction across multiple contexts, as manifested by the following, currently or by history.
2. Restricted, repetitive patterns of behavior, interests, or activities, as manifested by at least two of the following, currently or by history.
3. Symptoms must be present in the early developmental period (but may not become fully manifest until social demands exceed limited capacities, or may be masked by learned strategies in later life).
4. Symptoms cause clinically significant impairment in social, occupational, or other important areas of current functioning.
5. These disturbances are not better explained by intellectual disability (intellectual developmental disorder) or global developmental delay. Intellectual disability and autism spectrum disorder frequently co-occur; to make comorbid diagnoses of autism spectrum disorder and intellectual disability, social communication should be below that expected for general developmental level.

For more detailed information, take a look at information by the Centers for Disease Control[4] and if you want to delve into this even farther, you'll find this link[5] helpful.

∼

The diagnosis does not tell you who your student is. It suggests that he might experience a range of characteristics. You will need to get to know him to see how these play out for him.

Your autistic student is not a cluster of symptoms. He's an individual with interests, strengths and challenges. And he needs your support in ways that will truly help him. You can do this.

Autism is a spectrum, but not a clear spectrum where some individuals fall at the extreme range and some at the mild end. It is much more complicated than that and fluid. Please read this excellent article, It's a Spectrum Doesn't Mean What You Think [6]by C. L. Lynch.

AUTISTIC STUDENT OR A STUDENT WITH AUTISM?

H ow should you describe him - as a student with autism or an autistic student? This is quite a controversial question with feelings split strongly into two camps. First, let's look at the "person-first" viewpoint. It began in the 1970s with the disability rights movements. This view espouses that the individual is a person first and autism is just a part of what makes him who he is, just as is having blond hair or being left-handed. He's a child first like any other child but with the add-on of autism.

This person-first language is used by most professionals - therapists, educators, etc. It is likely what you were taught when you took your teacher training.

The aim is to see the child first as an individual, rather than focusing on the label. This is meant kindly and it's a reaction to the time decades and decades ago where we lumped kids together according to their labels. Nowadays we would not describe someone as a "cerebral palsy child" but "a child with cerebral palsy", with a visual impairment, etc.

By focusing on the person rather than the disability, the hope is to reduce assumptions, generalizations and stereotypes. Often when parents receive the diagnosis about their child's autism the news will be couched in person-first language. Most professionals practicing today will have been trained in this language. Here[7] is a handout on this put out by the US Centers s for Disease Control on using person-first language. DisabilityisNatural.com[8] gives you an explanation about the benefits of using person-first language and a series of articles demonstrating this point of view. There is merit is paying attention to what the individual says. This short video collection[9] features young people who prefer person-first language.

~

I n contrast, there are many autistic people who adamantly support the use of identity-first language. They say that they are autistic. To them, autism is not an add-on, but an integral part of their neurology. The "with autism" implies that it's something extra or even bad. They claim their identity firmly. The movement for identity-first is so strong that those not using it on some social media sites will get called out.

This is worth thinking about. To get some perspective, here are a few sites to check out on this important debate:

A utistic Self-Advocacy Network.[10]
  •8 Reasons Why You Should Re-Think Person-First Language.[11]
  •"Autistic Person" or "Person with Autism" - Is There a Right Way to Identify People? [12]
  •A survey asking disabled people which language they preferred.[13]
  •Neurodivergent Rebel's video on the language debate.[14]
  •Autism *Actually* Speaking.

As you can see, there are very strong beliefs on either side of this debate. Throughout this book I have used both terms.

When talking to someone who has an autism diagnosis, why not ask them which they prefer? Often this means going with the preference of the parent. If the child is old enough, give him or her the choice. Ask which he prefers. And, be prepared for this choice to change as the child matures and learns more about his identity.

WHAT CAUSED HIM TO HAVE AUTISM?

⚜

A h, this is something parents ask a lot, especially those with a newly diagnosed child.

First, it's not their fault. They did nothing to cause this difference in their child. It happens.

∼

S ince autism is so prevalent, a lot of effort and funds are going into the possible etiologies or causes of autism. Most agree that there is a genetic component to autism. While not directly inheritable, there is a stronger incidence within some families.

If you hear that autism has a genetic basis, often we think of something inherited. But, "if you have one child with autism, the risk for the next child is only 2 - 6%. If autism were due to a single gene, we might expect numbers like 25% or 50%." The article at this link[1] talks about some of the genetic studies done with families who have and don't have children who are on the autistic spectrum. In some cases, the children share the same genetic abnormalities of their parents, even when the parent does not have

9

a diagnosis. Other times the child's genetic pattern shows a duplication or gene deletion.

There are some interesting theories about early brain overgrowth; you can watch an easy to understand explanation of this here[2].

Either way, this is not something the parent could control.

But Why?
There are several schools of thought about the research into the cause of autism. Some people would like to know what causes autism so that it can be prevented from happening. Many parents and teachers are in this camp - it hurts to see your child struggle and we'd all like life to be as smooth as possible for our children.

Other people feel that there is only so much money to go around. It's a fact that we have autistic kids. Rather than funding research into a cause, they would rather that money go toward effective treatments to make life easier for the kids and for their families.

～

Here's one way of thinking - *if you can't make it not happen, make it go away.*
While you might have some sympathy for wanting it all to just go away, especially on those bad days, articulate, autistic adults take great exception to this. Think about it. Trying to eradicate autism makes it seem like you are trying to get rid of those who *are* autistic. What value are you putting on their lives? There are many autistic adults who are happy. They like themselves. Sure, most freely admit to the struggles they have had and still do have, but they think they are okay.

Put yourself in their shoes (or in the shoes your student will one day wear). Autism in many ways defines their lives; it is not an add-on to their way of being - it *is* their way of being. Then listen to people wanting to stamp out autism, to eradicate it from this world. Imagine how that would feel. (Like it's a form of genocide). Now you might understand the resentment many autistic adults hold for those organizations they perceive as wishing to banish their existence from the face of this earth. How does that jibe with those autistic adults who like themselves, enjoy their life, despite their struggles, and feel that they have something to offer the world?

The wanting-it-to-go-away at all costs has led to some potentially dangerous practices. Think long and hard about having your child ingest substances that are reported to "cure" autism.

~

Some parents might say, "My child will never be like those adults." Perhaps, but who knows? Never assume. The way that child is now at age three, will resemble little the adult he will become. Who knows how he will develop? Do not write him off and do not set limits on his growth.

Yeah, easier said than done. It's hard when all the other kindergarten kids are running around, chatting to friends and approaching each new task with enthusiasm, but that one child does not want to leave your side. He does not speak. He does not appear to even notice the other students.

Again, don't assume. Just because he does not seem like he is aware of his surroundings does not mean that he is oblivious. In fact, he may be hyper-aware, taking in everything at once with an intensity the rest of us could only imagine. His little body could be bombarded with input he is struggling to manage without being totally overwhelmed.

It's tough when a child does not talk - tough on his family and teachers but even tougher on him. But not being able to speak is not the same thing as not having anything to say.

Yes, speech is likely the easiest and most direct way to communicate but when this option is not available, there are other ways. Many parents of nonverbal kids develop a sixth sense as to what their child seeks. Most develop elaborate systems of pantomiming, pointing and trial and error. It's one thing for the parent to intuitively understand their child after hours and months and years of being with him. But you? You've just met him this year and he is one of two dozen little bodies in your room. Frustrating for you? Yep. Frustrating for the child? We can only imagine. We'll go into communication more in the chapter What If He Can't Talk.

Please, please, do not talk about your student in front of him. Some people assume that because a child does not talk, he cannot understand your words.

Autism happens. It's no one's fault. Get over it and get on with it.

IS AUTISM SOMETHING HE'LL OUTGROW?

The short answer is no. He won't grow out of it and there is no way to make it all go away. If your student has autism, he will always have autism.

But that does not mean that the way he is right now is the way he will always be. Of course not - no one is. We all grow and change and acquire new skills. The rate at which we learn, and the depth of that knowledge will differ but everyone can and does learn. This most definitely includes your student. But, in the words of Temple Grandin, "Once autistic, always autistic."

Is that a bad thing? Some, especially some autistic adults would say certainly not. They like themselves. They may view and interact with their world in ways that differ from that of neurotypical people, but different does not mean bad or wrong. It's just, well different.

We all know that being different can be hard. Not following the norm can be rough. True. Must it be that way? Perhaps we can play a part in making neurodiversity mainstream and acceptable. Maybe it is not the autism that makes it difficult for some to navigate this world, but rather how the rest of us respond.

In the neurotypical world there is the assumption that we all like roughly the same things. The noise and the lights, smells and crowds are just part of life that we pay little attention to. Most of us are able to block out those extraneous things to get done what we need to do. But what if your senses were acutely aware of sounds, smells, lights, colors, pressure, etc.? What if a trip to the mall felt like torture, leaving you drained for hours afterward? That's how it feels for many autistic people.

Have you heard about quiet shopping? Some stores are becoming more aware of the sensory challenges that may affect some customers so are holding quiet hours for these shoppers and their families. During these times, the lights might be dimmer, the music is turned off, there will be no loud announcements, and similar things. Sometimes these quiet shopping times are outside of regular store hours so there will be fewer people around. Small changes like this can make the world a more welcoming place for those with autism. And, autistic individuals are not the only ones with sensory sensitivities. They are common with sensory processing disorders, fetal alcohol syndromes and many other conditions.

∾

B ack to our original question. No, that student will not outgrow autism, but he will learn and mature. The autism he displays at age four may look very different than at age fourteen or twenty-four or forty. But, it will not go away.

Would the world be as it is without the contributions autistic individuals have made? Maybe not. Referring again to Dr. Temple Grandin, she suggests that neurotypical cavemen would have been sitting around the campfire socializing while the autistic types went off and invented new ways of doing things. Listen to her talk on The World Needs All Kinds of Minds[18].

There is no "cure" for autism but there are ways to assist the child to navigate his way in the world.

Read what these autistic adults say about Things We Love about Being Autistic[19].

DO I HAVE TO ARRANGE MY WHOLE CLASSROOM FOR JUST THIS ONE CHILD?

No. That is the short answer.

But, can you or should you ignore his needs? No. You went into teaching to teach and to reach kids. That means all kids, even those whose ways of viewing the world are different than yours.

I've heard things like this from teachers:

- I run an academic program.
- He doesn't belong here.
- My year is already planned out.
- This is the way I teach, and the students need to adapt to it.
- It's too much work to do things differently.

What would happen if you try to pretend that that autistic student is not there? What happens if you carry on as if that child with dyslexia is not sitting in your room? Or, the child who struggles with attentional issues? Odds are that neither of these kids will simply sit there quietly, allowing you to continue teaching in your preferred fashion, without interruption.

Bad things happen in a classroom when your kids are not engaged in your lessons. (You know what I mean).

So, first, it is your job to teach each and every one of the kids who cross your doorway, no matter what their learning style, ability or academic standing. Second, if you don't work at including them, your classroom behavior management skills will likely be taxed, plus you'll lose valuable instructional time while trying to keep order.

When you accommodate, when you make that student who has additional needs feel included, valued and successful, not only are you helping him to achieve, teaching all the students to appreciate differences, but you're actually making your life easier in the long run.

It's hard. Yep, it is. I'd say, "That's why you're getting the big bucks," but that's not exactly true, is it? You're a teacher and teachers teach. Yes, initially it can be more work to look at your lesson plans and tweak them in ways that will make your messages more accessible to more of your students. Take a look at this "Autism Advice for Teachers[20]".

Here's the good news. This does not mean that you need to set up a separate program for each student who is "different" in your room. Luckily, many of the strategies that will help your autistic student will also benefit many other pupils in your room.

Take visuals, for example. Visual strategies will benefit students who have autism, learning disabilities, fetal alcohol syndrome, attention deficit, central auditory processing weaknesses and many more kids who do not have a formal diagnosis.

Not relying solely on auditory methods to get your information across will also positively affect a variety of students. Allowing kids to demonstrate their learning in a variety of ways will help keep kids engaged and meet the needs of many in your room.

. . .

S omething as simple as how you set up your classroom can make a big difference for your autistic student and for many of the other kids in your room. The way you decorate the room can impede learning. Think about that. Those of us who took our teacher training back when the earth was cooling, were taught to make our rooms bright, colorful and full of things to snag our pupils' attention. We know now that that type of engagement is not what we want. Here are some Dos and Don'ts of Classroom Decorations[21]. Part of this has to do with executive functioning and part due to sensory sensitivities. Here are some of the sensory challenges of students[22].

K eep in mind that you are only thinking about these things in terms of your autistic student, but also for many of the diverse needs within your room. You will also meet kids whom to you seem to display autistic characteristics but don't have a diagnosis. (And, they might never receive one because seeking a diagnosis is a parental decision). The environment you create counts more than the diagosis. Here are 3 Golden Rules for Supporting Autistic Pupils[23].

∾

S ometimes what we think is best for a student is not actually what they really need. Ask your student. Talk to his parents and former teachers. And, listen to those autistic adults who have been where your student is now. They are in the best position to offer you advice. Here is an article on Letting Go of Control and Rethinking Support for Autistic Individuals; Compliance is NOT the Goal[24].

∾

I n our schools we can appreciate human diversity. We model to our kids the way we feel about those who have brains wired differently and who learn differently. Human diversity should be celebrated, not treated as a disorder. [25] Do you try to fit the child into the environment or alter the environment to fit the child? In the long run, the latter will be easier on you.

Dr. Temple Grandin is likely the most famous autistic person in the world. She was nonverbal until school age and acted very autistic. Doctors told her mother to place her in an institution. Now, she's a university professor, has written numerous books and speaks in many countries, advocating for autistic kids and different kinds of minds. Here is her presentation on The World Needs All Kinds of Minds[26].

Listen to what Debra Jenkins says about "Normal....Is a Dryer Setting"[27].

We need to "Make Differences Ordinary in an Inclusive Classroom"[28].

WHY IS HE NOT LIKE AN AUTISTIC STUDENT I HAD BEFORE?

No, he is not like that other autistic student you had, is he? It's a shame, isn't it? They both are autistic, but different. By the end of that previous school year you sort of had that other student figured out. Now, it feels like you are back at square one.

If it is any consolation, your current student is probably thinking the same thing. He wonders why you are not like the teacher he had before. You are both women, brunette, teachers, gliding toward middle-age, and working in the same school. In fact, your classrooms are even on the same side of the hallway. But, from his point of view, sadly, your routines and expectations differ. Drats! And it had taken him ten months to get into the swing of things with that other teacher. Now he is once again in that uncomfortable place where everything is new, and he does not know what will be expected of him.

J ust like you are both teachers and that is a defining
characteristic of your lives, both this student and your
previous one have a diagnosis of autism. That means that
during the diagnostic process they both met certain criteria.

There are certain hallmarks of autism that each individual will
have to a greater or lesser degree. This is why two kids will not
present in the same fashion.

Like with all the following traits, there are not hard and fast
rules that you can use to generalize. You need to get to know your
student and how they play out in his life.

An excellent online site, The Aspergian, [29] describes seven
characteristics that those with autism have, to greater or lesser
degrees. They are:

- Pragmatic Language
- Social Awareness
- Monotropic Mindset
- Information Processing
- Sensory Processing
- Repetitive Behaviors
- Neuro-Motor Differences

I t's worth taking a look at them in more detail here[30].

C ompared to your typical students, an autistic child will have
difficulty with communication. For some, they might be
nonverbal (you might want to look at the chapter that deals with
nonverbal communication). Other autistic kids are highly verbal
(take a look at the chapter called What If He Talks Too Much?).

Despite having good verbal skills, that child can still have language difficulties. There is a difference between having a great vocabulary and speaking fluently and easily understanding what is said to you. A great many autistic kids will have difficulty with auditory processing, making sense of the words that they hear.

Although he may be able to use those exact words you said in a sentence of his own, attaching meaning to your words may not be an easy task. (We talk more about auditory processing in the chapter dealing with auditory sensitivities). Just keep in mind that understanding what he hears may not be as easy as you would assume. And auditory processing skills worsen in noisy, confusing or new environments.

A long with this comes processing speed. Struggling to make sense of what he heard might take time, more time than you would expect. If you interrupt his processing task, he may need to begin all over. While his brain is processing what it heard, you may be waiting for his response. To you, that ten or twenty second wait can seem long and uncomfortable; he likely won't notice the passage of time.

Slow processing speed might not be apparent just with auditory processing. Beginning tasks and switching focus and ending tasks can also take more effort and time than with neurotypical kids. Part of the reason for this might have to do with executive functioning skills and monotropism. (Check out the chapters on attention and on executive functioning).

Take a look at A Day in the Life of a Child with Slow Processing Speed. [31]

F ine and gross motor coordination are often areas of weakness for autistic kids and can play a part in slow processing. When the act of holding a pencil isn't fluid and requires concentration and effort, the act of writing can be a challenge. Watch how your student holds a pencil. He might be gripping it tight enough to turn his knuckles white. Think how tiring that would become after just ten minutes.

Sitting upright in a desk requires good trunk muscles; some autistic kids have low muscle tone, making holding their body up tiring. You may notice them slumping and changing position often.

The pathways may become clogged or sluggish when sending messages between knowing what they would like their body to do, and their brain sending the impulses to those muscles needed for the job. Amanda Baggs demonstrates this well in her short video clip *How to Boil Water the EASY Way*[34].

A lmost every autistic kid will have difficulty with social communication. Social communication involves those subtleties of our language and our culture that we almost never think about teaching children; they just pick these things up almost by osmosis. But this seems to not come readily to most autistic kids.

There will be difficulties with pragmatics, the social niceties of language as well as the nonverbal communications involved in facial expressions and body language. (We talk more about this in the chapter on social understandings).

S ensory issues plague most autistic people to a greater or lesser degree, depending what other pressures are on them. Some autistic kids are on high alert all the time as their body works at fending off invading sensory sensations. For other autistic kids, this recedes somewhat and only becomes exacerbated during times of stress. We talk more about the sensory aspects of classrooms in the specific sensory chapters. I would strongly suggest that you read them; you might be surprised at just how much sensory inputs affect your student.

S ome autistic kids have enhanced visual perception. They derive meaning readily from things that they see. They might have a wonderful visual memory. (If that is true of your students take advantage of that mode of teaching).

~

E ach autistic student is an individual with a unique profile of strengths and challenges. Take a look at C.L. Lynch's article, It's a Spectrum Doesn't Mean What You Think[32].

WHICH PROFESSIONALS MIGHT
BE INVOLVED?

Many in your profession teach for years without close encounters with those other, non-teaching professionals school districts often employ. Some of these people might be involved in gathering information that can lead to a student's diagnosis; others will step in after the diagnosis. They might provide individual or group therapy or consult with you on strategies that would be helpful in the classroom. Sometimes these professionals might be employed by your district and sometimes they may be contracted for certain hours or tasks.

And, sometimes parents will pay for private therapy. They may want that therapist to come into the school. Check with your school district before you agree to this. Often schools have strict policies on who can enter their buildings. There might be a requirement of first having a criminal record check, etc.

Then there is the potential for conflict. What if this therapist wants to come into your room? While *you* and other school personnel have the right to be in that room and interact with your students, there could be a confidentiality breech if this non-school person observes other children in your room. What if this therapist the parent brings in suggests that you use certain approaches in your room that make you uncomfortable or don't fit with your philosophies? Although you don't want to appear uncooperative with the parents, please involve administration before meeting with or working with professionals not associated with your school.

~

If a child is newly diagnosed, the parents might come to you with questions. Once the reality of a diagnosis sinks in there is often a mad dash to find the professionals who can help. You don't want to dash these parents' hopes, but here is a fact they need to hear - no matter how hard they look, no matter how much money they (or the school district) spends or who they find to be on the team, no one can make the autism go away. Seriously. If someone tells you that they can "cure" a child of autism, run and run fast. Either that person is purposely trying to mislead, sell false hope or they really don't know much about autism.

Autism is a life-long condition, a way of viewing and interacting with the world. This basic neurology will not go away.

But there are things that can be done to make life easier for your student. That is what you might hope to seek from professionals.

Let's look at who might be in your corner. Autism is a social communication disorder. This applies to every autistic kid, even those who seem to be highly verbal as well as those who are not speaking at all. A group of professionals you might find useful are speech/language therapists. For just a minute, we'll discuss some of the titles they might go by:
- speech/language therapist (SLT)
- speech/language pathologist (SLP) - speech therapist
- language therapist

- speech and language therapist (SALT)

In North America, the title speech/language pathologist (SLP) is commonly used: in Britain, speech and language therapist (SALT) is heard frequently.

A **speech/language pathologist** is someone who has spent a number of years at university or college - often at least five years. They might have taken undergraduate classes in language development, psychology, child development, neurology, physiology, anatomy, etc. while getting their bachelor's degree. In most countries this is not enough education to be a practicing speech/language therapist and they must take a couple years more training to get their master's degree. Some will carry on attaining doctorate degrees although that is less common.

These years at school focus on typical speech and language development, atypical development, acquired communication difficulties (such as through head injuries, strokes, etc.), social communication, pragmatics, assistive technology, apraxia and articulation, to just name a few of the areas. Some SLTs branch off into audiology where they specialize in the assessment of hearing and auditory processing. Their university training includes practical, supervised experience as well as internships before being licensed to practice.

When you mention the words speech therapist what sometimes come to mind is an adult working with a child who says "wabbit" for "rabbit". This is an articulation error and something that an SLP might work on. Some people are surprised when an SLP does not get all bent out of shape about a small child's lisp or articulation error. Some such errors are not unusual in kids of a certain age. Here [32] you can find information on the speech sounds and language skills that are typical for various ages.

SLPs work on both speech and language. Speech is how we say words and encompasses such things as articulation, fluency and voice. Although the speech area is the one we might be most familiar with, SLPs also focus on language. Language is divided into two main areas - receptive and expressive, meaning how we take in language and how we express our wants, needs and ideas. On this page you'll find an explanation of both speech and language: https:// www.asha.org/public/speech/develop-ment/Speech-and-Language[33]. Your child might be showing struggles in one or both of these areas. It is common for autistic kids to have language difficulties.

Another area that SLPs might work on is social skills or social understanding. They are not the only discipline that is knowledgeable in this area. Psychologists, occupational therapists, counselors and educators also work on social understanding. This is a good thing that so many professionals take an interest in social understanding for it is a realm full of challenges for autistic individuals.

~

Another professional who might help is an **occupational therapist**. Like SLPs. These are therapists that have spent at least five or six years in training at university, including internships in various settings. OT's can assist in a variety of ways. Here's what the Canadian Association of Occupational Therapists[34] has to say about their work:

An occupational therapist will try to find out why a client cannot do what they would like or need to do. An OT may check:

• your physical abilities like strength, balance and coordination,

• your mental abilities like memory, coping strategies, organizational skills

• what materials or devices you use to participate in activities, like needed furniture, utensils, tools or clothes,

• which social and emotional support is available to you at home, school, work or in the community, and

• the physical setup of your house, classroom, workplace or other environment.

S ome OTs have additional training focused on sensory issues. We discussed sensory challenges earlier in this book. An OT can be helpful in identifying which sensory areas may be impacting your child's life and where he is under-responsive or over-responsive. They can also help the cooperation cope with these challenges, reduce some of the extremes and help him or her to better self-regulate.

This is huge! Many of the behaviors that are most troubling could have a sensory basis and any help you can get in this area will be very welcome.

OTs also assist with the tasks of daily living - everything from eating to dressing to using the bathroom and navigating their world. Although every OT practice differs, here's a short video clip [3]of how one OT group works with kids and families.

∾

P sychologists might also play a part in helping your child. These professionals have either a master's level or doctorate level degree in their field. Psychologists are often involved in the diagnostic process. Part of the diagnostic criteria specifies whether or not the child also has an intellectual disability; this is the domain of a psychologist. But their role need not end with simply an IQ test.

Anxiety is something that plagues many autistic children and adults. They might even have a separate diagnosis of anxiety disorder. The anxiety might stem from sensory issues, understanding the social world, feeling different or trying to fit into their world, etc. But it's still anxiety and if you have ever experienced anxiety, it is not pleasant to say the least. A psychologist might be one of the professionals who would help your child learn ways to manage anxiety. They might do it through desensitization, cognitive behavior therapy, relaxation techniques, and build on the child's social understanding or many other ways that would be appropriate to that particular child. The therapist might also work with you on ways to teach an anxious child.

Psychologists might also look at adaptive functioning - how well your child manages in his world compared to others his age. Kids who have intellectual disabilities are usually behind their peers in the self-help and independence areas of adaptive functioning. But some bright autistic children may also lag in adaptive functioning or have scattered results where they are on par with their peers (or even above them) in some areas but be delayed in others.

These adaptive functioning skills are things that an occupational therapist or a psychologist may help with.

You might think that there is some overlap, and you would be right. Psychologists, OTs and/or SLPs might all run groups or individual sessions that build your child's skills in understanding the social world. Some might be called social skills groups; others work more on social understandings to help your child navigate his world.

～

Social workers are another group who might offer some assistance. While there are social workers whose jobs focus on child protection and some on financial aid, others fill counselling roles. They might work independently with your child or on a team with some of these other professionals.

～

There are large groups of people who call themselves therapists or counselors. Depending on where you live, some will be licensed and some not. Some will have university training in their field; some will have training in varying lengths from a weekend course to several years of study in one particular approach.

To parents, this is a bewildering, new world and they are inundated with information. They may approach you for advice.

You don't have the final decision and you don't want to be responsible for their choices. Here are a few general suggestions that you can give them.

Get references. Are other parents pleased with the results when this person/organization worked with their child? Is there data-driven evidence that this approach works? What is the cost? If they are asking them to take out a second mortgage on your house, be leery.

Do they promise a cure? If so, run. Autism is not something that goes away. Their child will learn and grow and acquire skills, but he will always be autistic, even when daily functioning becomes easier. Do they promise that by a certain age he will be "indistinguishable from his peers"? Again, the autism will not go away.

Does the approach respect the child for who he is as a person? Will he be made to feel badly about his natural likes and inclinations? Does it just want to change him? Will this approach fit into their family's lifestyle, beliefs and budget? Is there the potential for physical harm? Mental harm? Is it developmentally appropriate? Think about how other kids his age learn. Is it natural for a three-year-old to sit at a table for eight hours a day? Children learn through play and they learn best when they feel loved and accepted.

∾

Despite the myriad of professionals who might offer assistance, the parents will not be taking their child to someone else who will "fix him". He's autistic; that won't go away and that's okay. What they and you are looking for are ways to help your student be more comfortable in his environment, be better able to manage himself, to follow his dreams and to thrive. How is that different from what you want for any of your children?

IS HE HIGH OR LOW
FUNCTIONING?

W hen you learned that you'd be getting a student with an autism diagnosis, there is a good chance that the terms high functioning or low functioning were included in the discussion.

While the DSM-V, the manual diagnosticians in North America most often use, does not cite these terms, the DSM does classify autism as Level One, Two or Three. These levels refer to the amount of support the child will likely require throughout their life with Level Three predicting the greater amount of support needed.

Say the child's diagnosis included the qualifier of Level One, without an intellectual disability. That means that his IQ fell within the average range or above. Many would then deem that child as "high functioning".

To psychologists and many educators "high functioning" refers to intelligence level. "Low functioning" would imply that that child has an intellectual disability (scores below seventy on a standardized IQ test). But it's not that simple with autism.

For one thing, it is easy to assume that a child who cannot talk has an intellectual disability. This is not a safe assumption to make.

(Look at the examples given in the chapters What If He Can't Talk?)

Autistic kids don't do well on standardized IQ tests. The way that they process information might not fit the norms of the test. They may do poorly on the timed sections. They may come up with out-of-the box solutions to the problems posed. Their answers to the verbal questions might not be succinct or what the examiner was seeking.

Then there are autistic people who might score quite well on the IQ test but have difficulty managing the demands of their life, sometimes even more so than someone who might not have achieved scores nearly as high on the IQ test. Here is an excellent article on Why Intelligence Scores Do Not Predict Success for Autistic Adults[1].

How an autistic person functions can vary throughout their life, in different environments and under different stressors. The article *What About Functioning*[2] illustrates this well.

Because of this, functioning labels can be misleading. In other chapters we've looked at examples of autistics Carly Fleischmann and Amanda Baggs. Both of these women were considered "low functioning" and severely intellectually disabled until they were given the opportunity to communicate through typing. Then they were able to demonstrate their thoughts and all that they knew. In their case (and likely many like them) functioning labels did harm by creating assumptions about these women. For more on this, please take a look at this short piece: Functioning Labels: Why You Shouldn't Be Using Them[3].

If a person receives the label of "high functioning" there is the presumption that that person can manage well on their own. Accommodations might not be offered when indeed they would have made a vast difference in that person's life.

"The difference between high-functioning autism and low-functioning is that high-functioning means your deficits are ignored, and low-functioning means your assets are ignored," by Laura Tisoncik.

This concern about labels is raised over and over by autistic adults. Please Listen to Autistic People[38].

~

Why Intelligence Scores Do Not Predict Success for autistic Adults[36].

What About Functioning Labels: Why You Shouldn't Be Using Them[37].

Functioning Labels: Why You Shouldn't Be Using Them[38].

Most of all, do not assume.

WHAT IF HE DOESN'T LOOK
AT ME?

What is your goal? Do you want him to look at you or do you want him to listen to you? There is a fair chance that he may be able to do one of these things but not both at the same time. Or, at least not do them both well.

For most of us, this is hard to understand. Gazing into someone's eyes is almost ingrained in us from Infancy. Think of that baby nestled in its mothers arms nursing or taking a bottle. Chances are, before the infant fades into sleep, there will be lots of eye contact exchanged between him and his parent. This might not be the case if that baby is autistic. In fact, lack of eye contact is sometimes the first sign noticed that an infant might be on the autism spectrum. It's not that that child never looks at someone's eyes, but his glance might meet and then quickly slide off. Why is that?

. . .

In some parts of the world lack of eye contact is not as big an issue. But, in many western cultures, not looking into someone's eyes might make you seem to be uninterested, impolite, disrespectful or even dishonest.

Should we try to insist that autistic kids make eye contact? Before getting to that, let's look at some of the reasons why we *do* make eye contact.

Sharing eye gaze with someone can be a sign of joint attention and shared pleasure. A small child, wanting to show you the tower he has made with blocks, might look from those blocks to your face and back to the blocks again, signaling where he wants you to look. We use the same method of following eye gaze with children when we want to direct their attention to something. Words might not be needed as that child learns to look where we are looking.

Picture a classroom full of kindergarten children. Something unexpected happens and the children all freeze. They look to the teacher for her reaction. If she flaps her arms in a panic and howls, chances are hysteria will break out in the room. But if that teacher's face and body language remain calm, the kids will take their cue from her response and remain calm as well. That is, those children who watched the teacher and picked up on the nonverbal cues she was issuing.

Mothers are notoriously skilled at conveying messages through facial expression and body language. Ever seen a mother quell a fight with just her narrowed eyes, pressed mouth and hands on her hips? Her offspring know what that look, and stance mean, and they cease-and-desist their squabble.

We pick up useful information from looking at people's faces. There is an autism therapeutic approach that is based on this. It is called Reference and Regulate[39]. Never once in this approach though does the child hear the words "look at me". It is one of those play-based therapies aimed at increasing the child's engagement, social skills and self-regulation. You can watch some video clips about Reference and Regulate here[40].

B ack to your question. Should we teach autistic kids to make eye contact? I've met a number of children where this was the goal of their well-meaning parents and teachers. Those children were taught, often through a reward system, to gaze into the speaker's eyes. Not always, of course, but when you observe many of those kids, well they were being compliant, and their focus was on staring at someone's eyes. But that's all they were doing. The message that person was conveying was lost.

Autistic kids are often concrete, black and white thinkers. If you tell them that they must look at someone's eyes, they might obey you and stare with an intensity that makes the conversation partner nervous. That child will be following your instructions to the letter. They may or may not be able to process any of the words that person is saying. And, they might well be creeping out the speaker with their fixed stare.

If you instruct that child to look at the speaker only some of the time, be prepared for questions like these. "Exactly how often should I look at them? Once every five seconds? ten seconds? Thirty seconds?" And, "For how long do I keep looking in each one of those instances?"

S ometimes it helps to consider autism almost like a processing disorder where a person can only focus on one piece of incoming stimuli at a time. So, that child can look at you or take in your words. Multitasking is an executive functioning skill that is often a challenge for kids on the autism spectrum. Often, I have observed in a classroom where the teacher complains that her autistic student does not pay attention to her. Yet, once the oral part of the lesson is done, that same, seemingly oblivious child, might do the assignment just fine. Or, although that student did not appear to be looking at the teacher once during the lecture, when you ask him a question about the material, he can give you a decent, relevant response.

He was listening. Think about the skills of central coherence that we have mentioned in other chapters. Central coherence involves two aspects. One is being able to pick out of the environment the most important feature to attend to. The other aspect is closely linked - being able to let the myriad of small details recede and focus on just the big picture. Typically, autistic kids have trouble seeing the forest for the trees. Those individual details stand out so strongly that it's hard to get the gestalt of the situation.

Also related to central coherence is the amount of detail that child might garner from looking at your face. Rather than regarding your face as a whole, they might focus on the number of freckles on your cheek, the pores on your nose, the hairs of your eyebrow, etc. All these bits take time to process and may steal energy and focus away from your words.

B ut this child still needs to function in society and not everyone will understand why he doesn't demonstrate typical eye gaze behavior.

Some autistic people say that prolonged eye gaze isn't just uncomfortable, but it hurts. The intensity can seem too much. Other autistic people say that to them it is intrusive and rude to peer into someone's eyes. We need to respect these feelings. You wonder though, could that actually be true? The answer would be yes, for some people.

Listen to what these articulate, autistic adults say about making eye contact. Carefully consider what they say before deciding if working on eye contact is an important goal for you, your student and his parents.

- How Autism Affects Eye Contact[41]
- Autism Eye Contact Must Know Info[42]
- Ask an Autistic: What About Eye Contact? [43]
- People with Autism Describe Why Eye Contact Can Be Difficult[45]
- You're Not Autistic You Make Eye Contact[46]
- Autistic Lack of Eye Contact: Normal Human Behavior [47]
- Autistic Traits: Eye Contact Avoidance[48]

If you don't feel like you can take my word for this, or more importantly, the word of autistic people, here are links to get you started reading some of the research:

- Why Eye Contact Over Stimulates People with Autism[49]
- Why Do Those with Autism Avoid Eye Contact? [50]
- For Those with Autism, Eye Contact Isn't Just Weird, It's Distressing[51]
- Why People with Autism Avoid Eye Contact[52]
- Why Some with Autism Avoid Eye Contact[53]

There are some tricks that might help. If that autistic student glances at the bridge of the speaker's nose, chances are no one will be able to tell that he is not looking at the person's eyes. Or, glance just at one eye from time to time. With encouragement from you, that student might feel comfortable explaining to the speaker that he *is* listening, but it's easier to concentrate if he looks away. The goal is enhanced communication, not compliance.

Here is a balanced video explanation by a therapist[15] with lots of practical suggestions.

WHAT IF HE CAN'T TALK?

Most of us who enter the field of education have good language skills and are highly verbal. Words and communication come easily to us. Just as we speak to our students, we expect them to talk back to us. But what if your autistic (or any other student) is nonverbal? The urge is to make his talking the goal.

Do you want him to talk or to communicate?

"Well, of course," you say. "I want him to talk and to communicate. They're the same thing." Well, not quite.

Speaking is one way that we communicate but there are many other ways. Teachers and mothers are the masters at nonverbal expression. Think back to when you were a child in grade five. Couldn't your teachers silence the class with just a look or body stance? Not a word needed to be spoken but the message was clearly communicated.

Although we can communicate ideas and wants through our facial expressions and body language, speaking is a straightforward way to convey messages. For most of us, it's easy, requiring little conscious thought.

But for those who are nonverbal or minimally verbal (more on that in another chapter), this easy-speaking option is not open to them.

Being nonverbal is not the same as not having anything to say.

I would appreciate it if you would read that sentence over again please. I don't know who first said that, but it is powerful. Please go back and reread that line.

Think about why we speak. We want our needs and wants met. We want to share ideas and express pleasure.

Say you have a student who may understand everything that is said to him and everything going on around him yet he is not able to form the words to tell you so. What you need to focus on then is a way for that child to communicate, to get his or her message across.

Can you imagine what it would be like to be unable to express your needs? Think about your student. Some of those unwanted behaviors might be just be due to frustrations in not being able to let you know what he wants or needs.

∿

Thinking and speaking are not synonymous. Do NOT assume that because a student is nonverbal that he is unable to think. The part of the brain which controls the ability to speak and the part of the brain which processes language are not the same. Broca area is responsible for forming and producing speech and Wernicke area is responsible for language comprehension

So, you ask, how can you help them to communicate? Well there are number of approaches from simple signing, picture cards to complex computer apps and programs. Especially for a young child or someone new to this system, consider a simple way to start and remember that this is a new skill you are teaching him.

Picture cards are one way to begin. Pick something that the child loves or often wants. Before giving it to him, show him the picture card of the object, pairing the picture with the actual object. Some of you with drawing skills might sketch the object. Those of us less talented might rely on ready-made line drawing cards. You can find a nice beginning set of such cards at http://do2learn.com/picturecards/overview.htm[54]. There is also a nice collection of symbols at Mulberry Symbols[55].

What do you do with these cards? Well, if the concept is new to him, you cannot expect him to "get it" immediately. He'll need to be taught through repeated pairings and explanations that this picture represents an object or activity that he wants.

For some kids, the picture of line drawing on the card might just be a squiggle with no meaning. If this seems to be the case, back up. Start with actual objects and pointing to them. Once your student is able to point to what he or she wants, you can try introducing photos of that object then later, drawings of it.

Giving a child a choice is wonderful but making choices is a skill that needs to be taught. Allowing a child choices gives him power.

These same pictures can also help the child understand and follow your classroom routines and schedules. You can see examples of these strategies in action at school and at home in the book, *Autism Goes to School*[59].

If communicating through pictures is new to this student, this might be a wonderful opportunity to partner more closely with his parents. Explain the concept to them, find out which pictures might be most relevant for their home environment, help them create these cards or supply them with sets. Some families display an array of pictures on the wall or fridge and the child can go pick one when he wants something or bring a picture to you demonstrate what he wants. And especially while you're in the initial teaching phase of this if he brings you a picture of a glass of juice glass, give him juice. If you can't quite picture how this might work, take a look here.

Some people couple these sorts of pictures with a story. Carol Gray first started the term "social story". You can learn more about social stories at this link[4].

A social story is a way of letting a child know what's going to be happening. If you make a social story don't assume it's a one-shot thing. It's good to read them over and over with a child.

Some people shy away from social stories, saying they're not writers or they're not artists. Doesn't matter. Trust me. My stick figures can portray a social story that kids understand. I tell them what the figure represents, and they believe me, for some reason. You don't have to have your pictures, or your social story printed out in full color laminated with borders etc. Nope, just something drawn on a napkin in a restaurant can often work. Try it.

If you live in a techie household and gadgets abound, there are dozens and dozens of communication apps you can put on your tablet, your phone or your computer. Some are quite complex such as Proloquo2Go[60]. It is an absolutely excellent program but (and you knew there was a but coming, didn't you?), it's very complexity can turn some people off in the initial stages. It is possible to use only simplified portions of the program if that's what suits your child's need, then as his skill level increases you can bring in more buttons and categories and choices. Again, this is a program that is excellent but on the pricey side.

If you do a search on the Apple app store or the Google apps store for communication apps, you will find a big array of them. Some of them will allow you a free sample or a temporary download while you try it out. I would definitely advise this because there's such a difference in them and some just might suit you and your child more than others. Many of them are under twenty dollars.

The apps will do something similar to what I was telling you about with the picture cards. There might be a series of pictures under the heading Drinks so a child would look through and see a picture of a glass that symbolizes the drink he wants. He would then touch the drink of his choice. In some programs he would show you his choice; others will speak that choice aloud, either as a single word or in a full sentence, including "please". You generally have a choice about the type of voice the program uses.

As the teacher, you can control the number of these choices. For instance, in a school setting that does not allow soda pop, you'd delete or not have soda as one of the choices.

Of course, you would also keep the number of choices quite simple initially while the child is learning. Many of these programs are robust enough that you could continue using it for years and are appropriate for adults. I will list a few examples of these in the Endnotes. They are by no means endorsements nor am I favoring one over the other but this is just to show you examples of what you might find out there. (You will likely come across the term AAC when you're looking at apps. AAC stands for Augmentative and Alternate Communication).

- Assistive Communication Apps in the iPad App Store[61]
- AAC Apps Review[62]
- Cheap, Easy-Use Augmentative Alternative Communication AAC Devices [63]
- Free and Inexpensive AAC Apps[64]
- Top Alternative and Augmentative Communication[65]
- Becca'sApp Reviews[66]

If your student is using a technological AAC at school, ideally, he would use that same system at home. Again, this requires close communication between you and the parents. There can be concerns about the device reliably traveling between school and home and back. Financial constraints might make it difficult for a family to afford such a device or app or software program. Sometimes grants are available, or service clubs can be helpful, but keep in mind the need to be respectful of the parents' wishes and feelings. Not all homes have computers or tablets, nor someone with enough tech savvy to deal with inevitable glitches. Even running out of batteries or losing a power cord can interfere with an AAC's effectiveness. Sometimes low tech is best.

Many parents are concerned about the amount of screen time their child has and, with very good reason. A concern about using an app on your tablet for communication is that that child could justifiably become glued to that tablet. It's one thing if a tablet is dedicated only for communication but it is another thing if that tablet is possessed tightly by a child who uses it mainly for gaming. I'm not saying that a child should never play games nor that she should not use a tablet, but this is a parental choice you need to keep in mind.

Those of you who might have backed away from using social stories due to concern over your story-telling or drawing ability are in luck in our technological age. There are a number of apps to help you out with social stories. We'll talk about just a few but search around; you'll find one you like.

Pictello[67] is a favorite of mine due to its ease of use for non-techie people. It's a visual way of creating social stories (and many autistic people are highly visual). Please take a look at it in action as a mom demonstrates how she and her daughter use it here[68].

One question parents (and some teachers) sometimes ask is if using some form of AAC will prevent their child from talking. The answer is a resounding NO! Think about it. If you are thirsty and want a glass of juice, what would take more time - saying, "juice, please" or grabbing your tablet, turning it on, calling up the app, swiping through until you found the icon for juice, pressing it and showing the tablet to your mom? In fact, often AAC acts as a bridge to the child developing speech. No, using AAC will NOT make your child loose motivation to speak. You can read more about this:

•AAC Will Not Stop a Person from Learning to Speak[67].

•AAC Does Not Hinder Natural Speech[68].

•AAC.[69]

•Effects of AAC Communication on Speech Production on Children with Autism[70].

In fact, AAC can have positive effects on speech and language development.

So AAC, whether a simple picture card, a robust app or a stand-alone communication device (such as Dynavox[71]) will not prevent your child from speaking. Of course, all these neat apps require power. Someone has to remember to recharge the device or keep spare batteries on hand.

Have you ever forgotten to charge your phone? You feel abandoned, don't you? But what if that device was your primary way to communicate with the world? The fall-out might not be pretty.

Some people worry about facilitates communication devices. Here are some of logical fallacies [19]and the necessity of presuming competence with your nonverbal students.

∾

A less techie option is sign language. A problem with using a tech gadget is that it runs out of juice. If your student uses sign language, he always has his fingers with him.

One thing that always bothers me is when a child learns sign language and uses it at school as his primary means of communication but no one in his house knows how to sign. Or, vice versa. To me that seems so isolating. So, if you are going to use signing as a way for your child to communicate please, please make sure that everyone in his environments learns how to sign as well, if signing is the agreed upon communication of choice.

There are a few different types of signing. Likely the most common is a ASL American Sign Language[72]. Another one is Signed English. The difference between the two is that in Signed English every word is signed and that includes the ifs, ands, buts, etc. It follows the spoken or written English exactly. In ASL some words can be grouped together to form a concept and every single conjunction and word of the phrase might not be signed as well. Far more people understand ASL than Signed English.

While ASL is fairly standard throughout North America, it differs somewhat from British Sign Language[73] although both use gestures, facial expressions and body language to communicate a message.

Makaton[74] is popular in the United Kingdom. It uses symbols and signs to support communication, following word order used in speech.

Sometimes kids who are autistic also have difficulties with fine motor coordination, or an additional diagnosis of Developmental Coordination Disorder, making it difficult for them to manipulate their fingers into the proper position for sign language. This can be frustrating for the learner and make it hard for the recipient to decipher what the signer tried to get across.

One solution to this might be baby signs; they usually require simpler finger movements and are designed to be manageable by very young children.

If you look online and do a search for baby sign[75] you will get lots of websites that show you simple basic signing. There is a lot of free information on the internet if you want to get started with baby signs. Many parents use baby sign with their children to help their kids communicate before they become verbal. It can be quite effective, and those parents think that it reduces the child's frustration and tantrums because they have a way to get what they want. That power really means a lot.

If you think that signing is something that might be helpful for your child, a speech therapist is the best person to guide you in which type. If you're raring to give it a try, you will find some useful information here[76].

～

One thing we have not talked about is apraxia[77]. Some autistic kids also have a diagnosis of apraxia or childhood apraxia of speech. It's also known as developmental apraxia or verbal apraxia. (Non-autistic children can also have apraxia).

An apraxic child will have ideas in his mind that he wants to communicate, but the messages his brain sends to his muscles in the mouth region do come across correctly. It's a problem of planning movement and carrying out movements. Apraxia ranges in severity. Here are some examples[78].

If your child is apraxic, will speech always be this hard for him? A qualified speech/language pathologist would be the best person to ask about your individual child. I can tell you though that of all the apraxic kids I have met, they have all been able to communicate through speech more easily over time and with therapy. This is something that an SLP can help with. You'll find more in the Endnotes at the back of the book on apraxia.

～

Let's circle back to the how we started this chapter. What if your student cannot talk? Speaking is our most efficient way of conveying information, but not the only way. And, not being able to speak does not mean that the student is not taking in information. Please do not equate being nonverbal with low intelligence. While there are definitely nonverbal students who have intellectual disabilities, it is *never* safe to assume that the two automatically go together.

It might be best to have some nonverbal people share their thoughts on this with you. Remember, the goal of speech is communication. Although they cannot speak how well do the following people communicate? What would have happened if teachers had made erroneous assumptions about them?

- Phillip[79]- "I have nonverbal autism. Here's what I want you to know."
- Ido[80] - Ido is a nonverbal autistic man continuing his education in college.
- Kaylie Clinton [81]- "Hear me speak without a voice."
- James Potthast [82]- nonverbal high school graduate writes a blog.
- Emma[83] - "I am an Autistic teenager whose body and mouth-words do not always pay attention to my bright and wise mind."
- Noah[84] - "Being nonverbal doesn't mean I can't think."
- Mike Weinstein [85] - once thought to be intellectually disabled.
- Carly Fleischmannn[86] - nonverbal young woman who has a YouTube channel.
- Amanda Baggs[87] - "About being considered retarded".

WHY DOES HE SPEAK SOMETIMES
BUT NOT AT OTHERS?

You might have a student who is "minimally verbal". For some of you this term will be new. Depending on the individual it's referring to, it can mean two things.

Some kids are not totally nonverbal - they do use some spoken language. They might say just a few, single words such as hi, bye, please, thanks, no, mom, dad, dog, more, etc. For most neurotypical kids, this is the way talking begins, with just a few key words then their vocabulary expands from there.

Even if they begin speaking later than their same-age peers, these few words can also be the beginning of being able to use speech to communicate and their expressive language abilities will continue to broaden from there.

For other autistic kids, their language might seem to get stuck at that stage, adding only some new words as the years go by. Often when a child begins to speak some words it's an encouraging step to more advanced vocabulary. But for some kids their language does not expand beyond a few words and phrases.

. . .

There are children with autism who do not tell their mom or dad when they want something, recite a story about their day nor respond when asked something. For much of the time they are nonverbal. Yet, that child might repeat word for word their favorite scene from a video. Or, rather than answering your question, an autistic child might repeat the question.

Frustrating? Can be, but it might be a way for the child to process what he heard and come up with what he wants to say. It could be a way to stall while they formulate a response. Another child might take pleasure in the sounds of certain words or phrases and repeat them over and over. Perhaps they soothe him or are a way to practice.

Have you heard of the term echolalia? Immediate echolalia is repeating what was said right after hearing it. Delayed echolalia may involve repeating something heard some time ago. People are often amazed at the memory of some echolalia kids who can accurately recite whole streams of dialogue from movies or conversations they've heard.

Some describe echolalia as "non-functional language". Hmmm. I am not sure about the non-functional part. Sure, echolalia to us is not a swift way of getting our message across, but to the person using echolalia, it might well perform a function. Here are a couple excellent explanations of echolalia. If your child has echolalia, please listen to these short videos.

•Here's an autistic opinion on echolalia[88].
•Ask an autistic - what is echolalia[89].

You will encounter autistic people who can carry on a nice conversation and tell you all manner of interesting things. From this you might assume that they are skilled in verbal communication. This may be true much of the time but under certain circumstances this ability may seem to become minimal or to desert them completely.

These circumstances often occur around times of anxiety, fatigue or sensory overload. When their system becomes so overwhelmed, they may lose the ability to speak.

Why, you ask? Again, hmmm. For most of us, this is hard to understand. Either you can talk or you can't. But it's not that simple for everyone. Whether or not it's politically correct, you may have heard the term "struck mute", referring to when something happens, and a person is at a loss for words. It's sort of like that, which could happen to any of us. But within a few seconds our ability would kick in and we could speak a coherent thought.

For some autistic people, when this occurs, they may be minimally verbal, able to get out just a few words or phrases. Or they could become nonverbal. Even though lots of thoughts are swirling inside their head, they can't get those thoughts out in words.

Consider just how frustrating this must be. And how terrifying. People who have previously heard them speak will wonder what's going on. They may accuse the person of purposely refusing to speak.

Think about school situations. An autistic child has intentionally or inadvertently done something wrong and the teacher is asking him/her about it. This is a child who usually speaks. But when put on the spot, the child remains silent. Sometimes from his face you can see the internal struggle going on. That could be interpreted as a child trying to figure out how to get himself out of trouble or as a child who is unable to form the words to explain. One is a normal kid thing, the other isn't. Refusing to explain could be seen as an act of defiance, getting the child in even further trouble, when in reality the kid could be so anxious and upset that the words simply won't come. Do you think that raising your voice, stepping closer or threatening consequences will change the child's ability to explain? Likely any of these actions would ensure that the child will be unable to express to you his thoughts of feelings for an even longer period of time.

Aside from the social and embarrassment factors of minimally verbal or nonverbal situations, let's consider the safety aspects. What if an autistic person is accosted by the police and cannot respond to the officer's questions or even give their name? What if there's a medical situation and the person is so distraught, they cannot give pertinent details? This is a time when an augmentative or assistive communication system would be vital. Something as simple as a piece of paper would work. If you want to learn more about some of the different communication systems, refer to the chapter What If He Can't Talk?

WHAT IF HE TALKS TOO MUCH?

While some parents would give anything to hear their child call their name or share a story with them, other parents would like a moment's respite from their child's constant talking.

This was often true of kids who had the diagnosis of Asperger's Syndrome. Asperger's was listed in the previous version of the DSM (Diagnostic and Statistical Manual of Mental Disorders), falling within the autism spectrum. Diagnostically it differed from autism in that the child did not have an intellectual disability and had no delay in acquiring spoken language. These children were sometimes referred to as "little professors" due to the way they would hold forth on topics that interested them.

With the revision of the DSM to the fifth version in 2013, the variety of labels under the autism umbrella were removed, simplifying the diagnosis to just autism, but with levels one, two and three, which indicate the level of support that individual might require and the caveat of with/without intellectual disability and with/without language delay.

Even if the label has changed, you will still know autistic kids who talk a lot. Why do they do this?

. . .

I t can interfere with teaching. During the school day, a child might share every thought bubble aloud. He might verbalize every thought and step as he works through a problem or assignment. I knew an autistic student who was fascinated with movies. His memory was phenomenal; you could say Clint Eastwood and he'd tell you every movie that actor starred in or directed, the year it was produced and so much more about each. He had an uncanny ability to related almost anything that is said in class to movies and would share this information freely, in exquisite detail and enthusiastically.

The interruptions were incessant, seriously hindering the learning of the group. Reminders and cues didn't work. Nor did explaining how this interfered with the lesson; he believed that sharing these movie facts was interesting and relevant (and he was right - some of it actually was). But, the time off-task was too great.

On his desk was a card with the word "movie". The word was circled with a diagonal line through the word. This was a visual reminder to not talk about movies during class time. Initially, the plan was that he was free to discuss movies with his teacher before and after class and at recess. But the teacher's time was then fully taken up with just this one student, leaving no time for private moments with anyone else.

The next plan was to provide a notebook dedicated to movies. Rather than talk about the movie tie-in, he was to write down his thoughts about it. This worked better as an outlet for getting out the movie trivia in his mind. (Unfortunately, this also meant that he was not listening to the teacher. On the plus side, his written language skills soared). He would still impulsively begin to share his movie knowledge but could be directed to write it in his book. The teacher would read (sometimes just skim) through his book and offer comments/feedback. This pleased the student.

Still, this wasn't enough. The administrator stepped in. She reinforced the ban on talking about movies during class. Understanding how tough this was for him, she set aside fifteen minutes of each day when he could be alone with her to discuss anything he wanted about movies. He loved his time with her.

While talking too much can interfere with your classroom, parents might complain to you about their child's incessant talking at home. You could refer them to this for suggestions to try[90].

W e don't teach typical kids how to converse with others; they seem to pick such skills up on their own. There is reciprocity to our conversations - person *A* talks for a few sentences, then person *B* takes a turn as the verbal ball goes back and forth. This is part of the social communication that does not come naturally to autistic kids.

Part of social communication is reading the body language and facial expressions of those around us. Again, this is something we rarely teach neurotypical kids, but these subtleties can be a mystery to autistic people. It's from reading these cues that we can sense when we have talked too much and are boring the listener.

When our conversational partner looks away, averts their head, dips a should down and away, shuffles their feet, etc., we realize that they are attempting to get away. At that point we can try to repair the conversation, to draw them in again by asking them a question, letting them have a turn to speak.

But if you don't have the skills to read these body signs, you would be apt to carry right on, especially when the topic is of great interest to you.

One of the diagnostic points for autism is "special interests". While most seven year olds know a lot about dinosaurs, an autistic child might have an encyclopedia's worth of knowledge on the topic. And be oh so willing to share that knowledge with you. These intense interests can be delightful and might lead into wonderful career possibilities down the road.

In the meantime, though, constantly hearing about that subject can be hard for those around. While the topic fascinates the speaker, those around him might be far less enthused. Besides the feeling of being lectured at wears thin.

I knew an adolescent who knew everything there was to know (or it seemed that way) about real estate in his city. Every Sunday he and his dad toured all the open houses they could find. This child knew about the history of local land development, housing values, zoning, you name it about real estate. And, he was oh so willing to share this information. While to a certain degree it really was interesting, the kids on the playground did not enjoy standing around listening to his lectures on real estate every day. They would simply leave; the boy did not understand why they'd abandon him and did not want to learn about this fascinating topic that he loved so much. When this is just the neatest topic ever, why wouldn't you want to share the information with others? What he saw as enthusiastically sharing, bored other people.

∿

Some people process information better when they speak out loud. The act of hearing the words helps to imbed meaning for them. There is nothing wrong with that strategy in some situations but when in the company of other people, it can cause problems.

Expressing thoughts aloud can interfere with the learning of others in a classroom or work situation. The noise might interrupt the concentration of those in the vicinity. When someone speaks our instinct is to pay attention to them, so ignoring them might be difficult.

During a test situation you can see how a child speaking out loud to himself could cause problems. Since it is a valid strategy and likely helpful to the child, that student might be better served by writing his exam in a quiet spot alone.

Subvocalizing is talking to yourself but at such a low volume that others may not be able to hear the words. Learning to subvocalize might help in situations where the person is not alone and free to talk aloud. Some kids learn to "talk in their head", still carrying out the dialogue but without speaking aloud. (Although better for those around them, it might not be as effective for the individual as it lacks the auditory feedback that might have assisted them).

Some autistic kids carry on a steady monologue while they play alone. Again, they might be using oral language to work through situations or practice skills, and it is not only autistic children who do this.

In this video clip, an adult autistic man discusses when he talks aloud to himself.[91]

And, what if he talks too loudly? This video[92] may help.

~

Even if your student has not picked up conversational skills on his own, you can teach him. Here are some resources that might help:

•Small Talk Can Loom Large: Teaching Your Child the Flow of Conversation

•Six Tips for Teaching Conversation Skills with Visual Strategies

•Teaching Conversation Skills

•Teaching Conversational Skills

•How to Teach Conversation Skills to Students with Autism

WHY IS HE SO LOUD SOMETIMES?

S ometimes an autistic student might be quiet and
withdrawn, while others might make more noise than any
of the other kids in your room. There are several things
that might be behind this.

We talked earlier about sensory sensitivities that might (and
likely do) affect your student. Those with auditory sensitivities can
find the noise levels in our classrooms quite irritating. It can be
rather like a water torture where the drip, drip, drip seems to get
louder and louder and more interfering. Maybe they can tolerate a
certain amount of the chatter and hustle and bustle first thing in
the morning, but by the time they've endured it for the last four
hours, well, they have just one nerve left, and everything is getting
on it.

In the auditory chapter, we looked at some ways you could help
lessen the noise load for your student. When you know that noises
bother him, why is he sometimes what seems like the loudest one
in the room?

When the noises are external, they bombard him, and he can
feel powerless against their assault. But, if *he* makes noise, he hears
that above the outside noises. The ones he creates are within his

control. He can hear his humming in his head, and it may drown out those annoying background noises. It doesn't have to be humming, but any vocalization might suit his purpose. He might not even be making a conscious choice to make his noises; it's an instinctive response to protect himself.

～

N oises he makes might be a vocal stim - part of the self-stimulatory behavior that gives him comfort. He might not even be aware that he is vocalizing. Unfortunately, his sounds might interfere with the learning of other students. If that is the case, are you able to provide him with a room or space on his own where he can make his noises without bothering other people? Is there a way of finding a substitute behavior that would still meet his need, but interfere less with those around him? When you're seeking possible substitutions, an occupational therapist or speech language therapist might have helpful suggestions. Think about what the sound is doing for the student. Does it mask other noises for him? Does he like the way the sound reverberates in his head? The way the sounds feel in his mouth? Is he repeating sounds, words or phrases in an echolalic fashion? Is he anxious and these sounds comfort him? If you have not read them yet, take a look at the chapters that deal with sensory sensitivities.

I know of one student who was aware of the noises he made and that they bothered those sitting near him. He felt entirely justified in what he was doing because so often the noise created by other students bothered him. Tit for tat. Noise cancelling earbuds helped him cope when the classroom was noisy, and he no longer felt the need to "get back at" his fellow students for the noise level in the room.

～

D oes he talk out loud in order to help himself process information? This can be a strategy used by students, including those who aren't autistic. Providing them a place where they can speak without disturbing others will help. Sometimes you can teach a student to subvocalize, speaking almost under their breath so that they can still receive that auditory feedback that helps them to make sense of words and ideas without being overheard by others.

～

K eep in mind that one of the diagnostic features of autism is difficulties with social communication. It is through acquired social skills that we learn to modulate our voices. Most kids don't need to be taught that while it's okay to shout and laugh loudly on the playground, once inside they must speak more quietly. It is be picking up social cues that kids learn to use voice levels appropriate to the situation. Students with autism are weak at picking up nonverbal social messages and may need things such as voice modulation specifically taught to them. Your student may be unaware of how loudly, or how softly he is speaking. A speech language therapist will have helpful suggestions.

Here are a few strategies to consider:

- Control-O-Meter [93]
- How to Get Children with Autism to Lower Their Voice[94]
- another How to Get Children with Autism to Lower Their Voice[95]

GIVE ME JUST ONE STRATEGY I CAN USE

❦

Tell me just one strategy I can do that will help my artistic student, help other children in my class and that won't overwhelm me.

There is actually an answer to that. Visuals. If you are only going to do one thing that might have the biggest bang for your buck, try visuals.

Most people who are autistic are stronger in the visual areas. They take in information that they see more easily than that which they hear. We talk elsewhere in this book about auditory processing difficulties and why relying on talking might not be your best approach.

Many of us who go into the field of education have strong language skills. Reading comes easily to us and more importantly, we are talkers. Even your time spent at university was a time heavily reliant on language skills. Right or wrong, I would imagine that many of the classes you attended were based on lectures. Someone would stand at the front of the classroom or lecture hall and talk at you. You would alternate between listening intently and madly scribbling notes.

When you reached the part during your teacher training where you were actually standing in front of a group of students most likely you spent much of that time talking. Talking comes easily to many of us and it is easy to fall back on the habit of lecturing.

But it is not only kids who have an autism diagnosis who may not be strong in the auditory area, meaning listening to your lectures might not be the most effective way for them to learn. Think about students that you have had who have attention deficit disorder. Think about students who have learning disabilities. Of those two groups, many don't do as well in a classroom that is heavily reliant on talking as the way of learning. From your classroom experiences you have discovered that there are certain kids who learn fare better when you have set up a hands-on situation. Rather than sitting nicely at their desk with hands folded giving you rapt attention while you talk and explain, some kids will learn more readily by doing rather than listening. And many will be more engaged in what you are doing if they don't have to just sit and listen.

As a teacher, have you ever had the experience where you stand in front of your class explaining in wonderful detail exactly what you want them to do and then asked them to get to work? But before you take one step away from your spot half a dozen hands go up. The kids ask, "What do I do next?" "What do you want us to do?" "What page was that?" "How many questions do we need to do?" And, the list goes on. You sigh and turn away so the children can't see your frustrated expression. You'd just explained what you wanted them to do. The words were hardly out of your mouth before some of the kids are questioning you.

Those are likely kids who don't take in information that they hear all that easily. Or kids who have attentional issues and, if their minds were distracted by something else, they were only half listening, and your words didn't register.

This is a frustrating situation that all teachers go through from time to time. But the answer is quite simple. Write it down.

Yes, whenever you give verbal instructions, pair them with

DR. SHARON A. MITCHELL

written directions, whether in words or pictures. Perhaps you want one corner on your board as the place where you always write the directions. It might be something simple like turn to page fifty-eight and do questions one to twenty in your math book. There will still be the odd child who will ask you what they are to do. But rather than repeating yourself over and over and over you could simply point to the board to that designated spot and direct the child's attention to where your instructions are written down. Over time, if you consistently use the same spot, your students will get to automatically looking there before they ask. That is one type of independence that you can foster in your children.

Another type of visual that will save you time and frustration, as well as helping your students, is to leave examples on the board. Leave sample math questions with the way you want a question handled. Leave sample sentences in your reading and writing area. You might have posters with examples of certain rules or theorems or grammar conventions. I know a couple of teachers who keep a binder for each subject at the back of the room. Within that binder there are tabs divided into sections. For example, in the math binder, there might be a section about addition, another about subtraction, another about multiplication or division etc. Within each section are examples that were used in the lessons. You don't have to be reinventing the wheel or making up all new examples just go with what you used already. The kids in the room have been trained that when they have a question, when they're not sure of how to tackle a problem, they are free to walk over to the binder, look through the correct section until they find examples of the problem they're trying to do. If they can't find the answer that they're seeking then they can go on to another problem-solving approach such as asking a neighbor for help, coming to talk to you, or looking back in their notebook to where they might have highlighted other examples.

One of the most helpful forms of a visual that you can use in your classroom is to have a visual schedule. How many times have you been asked, "what are we doing next?" On occasion, you can handle that question just fine but when it happens over and over across the course of the day it gets harder to remain patient. I found that a visual schedule is one of the things you can do that will benefit so many kids in the classroom plus help you from having frayed nerves.

The visual schedule will look quite different depending on the age of the students in your room. For kindergarten kids who are still non-readers, it would likely be a picture schedule. You can talk to the kids about which picture icon means music or circle time or recess time or bathroom break etc. These pictures don't have to be fancy and you do not need to buy an expensive software program to create them. You can find a number of pre-made visuals online or you can make up your own. One website that has a nice variety appropriate for school is www.dotolearn.com[96].

For kids slightly older you might still want to use the picture icons, but you might also pair them with the words as kids are getting into the early reading stage. Or, even if most of your kids can already read words but you still have a few who aren't at that level yet, keeping the picture icons, paired with the word, will be helpful. If you have very young students some might have difficulty recognizing what a line drawing represents; for those children, you might need to back it up a step and take photos. For example, if you wanted a photo that symbolizes circle time on the floor you might have all the children sit in their circle and then stand behind them and take a picture and use that. Or even younger children or some kids who have intellectual disabilities even the actual photo might be difficult for them to relate to for some kids you might need the actual object. For instance, if you want the kids to go get their crayons to work on some project rather than writing out the word crayon, having a line drawing of a crayon or taking a photo, you might tape or glue an actual crayon onto the schedule.

Again, depending on the age of the kids your schedule might

cover a full day or only part of the day. Older students can likely handle a schedule that would show what they are going to do during their whole day at school; some younger children might be only able to handle from first thing in the morning until noon or from the start of the school day to first recess.

Then, post the schedule someplace prominent where all the kids can readily see it. I know one young teacher who spent time making a schedule that she had beside the board for the first week then she moved it to the wall beside her desk. She did that because she found it extremely useful and she referred to it all the time. She said she did not have to open her planning book to see what was coming next, she could just look at her schedule. The problem was, where she moved the schedule to was out of sight of the children. It's great that it was a helpful aid for her, but the main point was doing something to help students not necessarily the teacher.

Other teachers leave it up for the first week and then they think, okay the kids got it, everybody knows what's coming next and they take it down. It's very true that the teacher has probably internalized the way their day will go and a few of the children will also have memorized the structure of the day. Those are the kids that are not concerning you though; it's those other kids who have not internalized it, those are the ones who need the visual reminder and they need ready access to it all the time.

I was once in a classroom where there was no large schedule for the whole class but there was a teacher assistant in the room, and she had a visual schedule. The teacher had made one for her because she was working with one boy who had an intellectual disability and another boy who was autistic. The teacher assistant used that schedule and she taped it to the inside of her own binder. She found it so helpful and sometimes when she wasn't clear on what was going to happen that day, she would take it out of her binder and put it on the wall beside her desk. She had ready access to it; the students did not. So, they would ask her what was going to happen next.

Make these available to the kids. Some students might benefit from having one taped onto a corner of their desk. Some might benefit from having one inside their notebook or a laminated copy that they keep in their desk that they can quickly pull out when needed. Apart from this, you should still have a large visual schedule readily accessible to all the students. But some kids who have attentional issues, visual processing images issues etc. might have difficulty looking at something that is far away from them. The bright colors of the shirts of their fellow students could interfere with what they are looking at, colors and movement could snag their attention so that even if they meant to look at the visual schedule, they don't end up seeing it or getting from it the information that they need. Such kids might do better with a near point schedule rather than relying on the far point access.

For some, especially students who do not enjoy school, enjoy certain subjects, or have a poor time sense, it can seem like the day is going to drag on forever. For those children you might have the picture or the word for the subject paper clipped onto the visual schedule or with loop and fibre. Once that subject is completed then that word or picture can be removed and put in an envelope for another day. It is all done and over with this is especially helpful if it's a subject that a student does not like they can see an end is in sight and then get on to something that would be more interesting.

Dr. Luke Beardon makes a good point. "Being autistic is not necessarily disabling," explains Dr Luke Beardon. "Instead, it is a disadvantage. And is that disadvantage a result of being autistic, or is it a result of being in a certain environment?" You can listen to his thoughts on this during this podcast[97].

WHAT IF THE PARENTS WON'T ALLOW ACCOMMODATIONS?

A s a teacher, you might see that a student is struggling; yet, your gut tells you that he can handle the material. That is where adaptations come in.

Most school districts will allow and even encourage adaptations. With an adaptation, you are not altering the curriculum. What you might be changing is either the way some of your students access the material, respond to that material and/or demonstrate their knowledge. Different regions might have different terms for this. Common ones are adaptations, accommodations, and response to intervention strategies.

Do you need to get someone's permission before you try such strategies? Often, that answer is no. But check the policies in your school. It never hurts to discuss this with other people as they may have ideas that you could try. Previous teachers may have found strategies that work for this child and can share their successes with you, as well what didn't work. But just because something did or did not work one year is not guarantee that that will hold true in the present situation.

What if you have some ideas you'd like to try that you think will help your autistic student? Do you need parental permission to do so? Again, check with your district's policies. Many will state that if you are altering the curriculum, this is not something you can decide on your own. Often, though, adaptations are within the realm of a classroom teacher's responsibilities.

If you observe in almost any classroom, you will see a teacher making adaptations. Some students require a more in-depth explanation; some kids need more practice. Some will confer with a group while others work independently. These types of Tier One strategies[98] are just part of our teaching practices. (If you're looking for more information on response to intervention, check out this link[99]).

~

Say you have a good handle on your autistic student's strengths and challenges and have been having success using various adaptations. Parent/teacher interviews roll around and you proudly show off his work to his parents, explaining how well he does with these strategies.

As you describe these approaches, you notice that his dad sits back. He crosses his arms and narrows his eyes. As your voice trails off, he leans forward. "Are you saying that my kid is stupid? Are you implying that he can't do the same work as everybody else?"

You back-pedal hurriedly, wondering where this is coming from. How could someone *not* want the method that brings out the best in their child?

Let's look at this from the parent's point of view. Back when they were in school (and perhaps during your years as well), every student in the classroom proceeded in lock-step fashion. Everyone did the same work at the same time. There were no accommodations and no allowances for differences. While *you* know that our views and knowledge about learning have grown and changed over the decades, adults not so involved in the education system have only in their minds what they experienced.

From a parent perspective, when you know that your kid is different, it's tough. We all want an easy, successful life for our children; realizing that things are going to be harder for your child is hard to come to grips with. If your child is autistic, likely he will have social difficulties and much of those school years are about socialization. An autistic child may act differently and do things that make him look different. It's easier if your kid will simply fit in but that is rarely the case with autism.

Knowing that people perceive their child differently, sometimes parents latch onto the one thing that might matter in school. His intelligence. There are autistic kids who also have an intellectual disability, but for the purposes of this chapter, we'll talk about students who are following the regular curriculum. (For more on this, skip to the chapter Is He High or Low Functioning?).

If your child is autistic and smart, the parent might want people to see his brightness and focus on that. Having a student do things differently can seem like you are watering down the curriculum because you don't believe he can keep up with his peers.

"Special ed" to some has been a dirty word with negative connotations of *those* kids off down the hall in a room of their own, never to rub shoulders with the rest of the school population. While inclusion is more the norm these days, adults not intimately familiar with modern schools won't know this. Anything that hints that his son will be in that "special ed" room will offend this dad. (I am not poking a stick at segregated classrooms; different individuals need different interventions at different times in their lives. Some students flourish in a smaller setting).

Autistic kids are often seen as less mature than their peers. While typical children have fewer and fewer outbursts once they're past the preschool years, over-the-top emotions might continue far longer in a child who has autism. Some parents might feel that their child needs to toughen up and suck it up. To them, that doesn't jibe with allowing accommodations that make it "easier" for him.

These parents might worry that you are mollycoddling their son and they fear that that type of treatment can't last. They know that once he's out in the world, he will be competing with kids just like those who sit around him in the seats in this class. And, in the work world, accommodations aren't there (that is changing, but slowly).

~

L isten to these parents. Heed the fears that are behind their words. Like you, they want the best for their child.

Now it's your turn to explain just what adaptations and accommodations are. Demonstrate how they are used all day long in your room (and the school) and not just for one or two students, but for everyone. Explain that you know their son can do the work and do it well, but he needs more time to put his thoughts onto paper. Show them just what their son can do when he is granted the time, he needs to do his best. Let them see the creative ways that their kid responds when he's allowed to demonstrate what he's learned in ways other than paper-and-pencil tasks. Reassure them that their son is following the regular curriculum and meeting the standards.

Chances are, the parents will be impressed with how well you've come to know their child and pleased that you think so highly of him. They might note that he does not come home from school as stressed as he once did.

W hat if the parents remain resistant and do not want you to continue with these accommodations? This is a time to rely on assistance from your administrator. If you and the parents feel it's appropriate, involve the student in these discussions. In my experience of decades as a school district consultant, only once have I seen parents not swayed by these arguments and examples.

An excellent resource for finding adaptation ideas is the wealth of material on the Vanderbilt University's Iris Center. [3] The materials are plentiful and geared to many adult learning styles. You can also share this link with parents.

~

T here is yet another scenario you might encounter. After getting to know a student, you suspect that he is showing signs of autism, yet there is no mention of this in his file. You learn that previous educators have also wondered about the possibility of an autism spectrum disorder. But, when this was mentioned to the parents, they want no part of this. They will not consent for a referral, for the gathering of data to support a diagnosis, nor will they look into it privately. They are upset that you would imply that there might be something "wrong" with their child.

What might be going on is that you have tapped into some inner fears they have had for a while now, worries that there might be something different with their child. They'd hoped that he'd grow out of it or that training would make it all go away.

Seeking an autism diagnosis is a medical issue. As the legal guardians, following this path is their choice. Maybe, in time, they will be more willing to look at the possibility, but they are not at that point now.

But their child is still sitting in your classroom and you want to do the best you can for him. It is possible to adapt successfully for him, whether or not he has a piece of paper confirming a diagnosis. After all, it's not the label that matters to you; it is understanding his strengths and challenges and determining the best ways to present information to him and to have him demonstrate what he's learned.

WHAT IS IT WITH THIS SENSORY STUFF?

$\diamond$

So, what's up with the sensory stuff you keep hearing so much about? Well, actually lots. In fact, sensory issues might just be behind many of the behaviors that you're seeing that aren't helping your student (or you or your classroom).

It's a rare autistic person who is not bothered by sensory sensitivities. As a school district consultant, when I'm called in to observe an autistic child who is struggling, my mind first goes to the sensory facets that could be impacting his self-regulation and his behavior.

$\sim$

Sensory issues in autistic people are not straightforward things. They can be either under-responsive or over-responsive to sensory input. Even more confusing, these do not remain the same. Under certain circumstance your student can be more sensitive than he might be at other times. And if he is in an environment where many things are coming at him, all the sensations could pile up on top of one another and make something that he could normally tolerate feel almost unbearable, culminating in a meltdown.

You might've heard the term meltdowns. A **meltdown is different than a tantrum**. All kids can throw a tantrum. A tantrum is when you are showing your displeasure about something that is happening or about not getting something that you want. Tantrums require an audience and if the audience goes away the tantrum subsides.

A meltdown is something different. A meltdown is not a child trying to get their own way or control their world. A meltdown is when that child has reached their limit; they cannot handle a single solitary thing more and are totally overwhelmed and then it all spills out. The way it spills out doesn't make your student feel good and it won't make those in the vicinity feel good either. So it helps when we can avoid or at least reduce the kinds of situations that will lead to a meltdown. No one wants to feel overwhelmed.

In trying to understand a meltdown, what leads to that state and how it might feel, it helps to hear the words from someone who has experienced this. Here's an excellent video on What are Autistic Meltdowns? [1]

And, if a meltdown does occur, it is not pleasant for the individual, nor anyone in the vicinity. Your goal will be first to keep that child and all others safe. Here are some tips on Autism Meltdown Safety[2].

~

Autistic kids spend much of their life in a heightened state of arousal. That is exhausting both for them and for the adults in their life.

We will address the sensory areas one at a time in the next chapters and in no particular order because there is no hierarchy of sensory needs for every autistic person. You can't assume that for the majority of autistic people, tactile will be an area that is highly sensitive. It varies from individual to individual, can change over time, and even within a single school day, depending on what else is going on.

Ideally, when a student's body is receiving the level of stimulation that it requires, he will feel calmer and more in control. Here[3] is a sample sensory diet form you can use as well as a list of sensory activities that might help your student's body to feel more regulated: https://www.understood.org/en/learning-attention-issues/treatments-approaches/therapies/download-sample-sensory-diet.

After reading the following chapters on various sensory aspects you might want to learn more about how they might affect your student. I would suggest that you keep in contact with the parents about this. They are the experts on their child and may be able to give you lots of helpful strategies that they have found work at home. When your student shows behavior that puzzles you, that you think might have come out of nowhere, think sensory and ask the parents for their thoughts.

You will also encounter parents who are not knowledgeable about sensory issues. This is sad and you are in a position to help. Understanding and accommodating a child's sensory needs will go a long way to helping that child be more comfortable.

～

If your school district is lucky enough to employ a occupational therapist, wonderful. Not all OTs have studied sensory processing but more and more have.. An occupational therapist trained in sensory matters would be the expert I would recommend you talk to, while you wait for an appointment here are some free, online questionnaires that might give you a place to start:

- Sensory processing assessment for adults https://www. sensory-processing-disorder.com/adult-SPD-checklist.html
- Sensory processing assessment for kids https://www. sensory-processing-disorder.com/sensory-processing-disorder-checklist.html
- •https://swishforfish.com/pages/nlc-sensory-learning-profile.
- Variety of resources: https:/sensationalbrain.com/free-resources.

I 'll bet that when you look through these links, your mind will spring to other students, both past and present, who do *not* have an autism diagnosis, but you recognize as likely being affected by sensory issues. You'll be right. It's not only autistic students who have sensory sensitivities. Kids with fetal alcohol syndrome and sensory processing disorder will have similar responses to stimuli as well as some students who do not have any formal diagnosis.

In the next chapters, we'll look at each of the senses individually.

TACTILE SENSORY SYSTEM

T actile has to do with the sense of touch. This really has two parts to it – one is feeling things with your hand such as fidgeting with something, and the other is how something feels on your skin. (The two are quite related though).

Sometimes people comment that an autistic child's behaviour changes with the weather. Possibly there is something to the theories about barometric pressure affecting people, but it could be something else. Some of you will live in temperate climates where the weather doesn't change much throughout the year, but for many people, there is quite a difference in temperature between summer and winter and, consequently, the clothing that we must wear.

Think about summer. For many that's a time when we wear shorts, sandals and short-sleeved T-shirts. There are large areas of our skin unencumbered, where nothing rubs. Then comes fall and often the start of school. That child who has been used to bare arms all summer, with the feel of the sun and the wind on them is now being forced to put on long sleeves and long pants. Jeans can feel heavy and scratchy and rub in not good ways. Those sweatshirts we put on kids are often loose and sloppy which makes them brush against your arms and your torso.

On the heels of fall comes winter when we might need to bundle up even more. It might mean putting on this piece of clothing that weighs heavy on your head, feels tight and constricting and pushes your hair against your ears and on your forehead. Suddenly people are trying to make you wear mittens or gloves - scratchy things on your hands, making it hard to feel and pick up things. Where your feet felt free and comfortable in sandals in the summer now, you're having to wear heavy, clunky boots.

The same difficulties can arise when the season starts warming up. Finally, that child has gotten used to the heavy, bulky clothing he or she was forced to wear all winter. Then comes spring and people are asking the child to remove the weight and the bulk that they have gotten used to. One little boy told me that when people wanted him to take off his winter boots, he feared he was going to float away outside because he was so light.

Think about that child who has become used to having his arms and legs covered, and then is expected to go outside in short sleeves. There's the feel of the wind on his arms, the sun on his skin.

Now, we can't all live in areas where the temperature hardly varies all year. We live where we live. And kids can get used to these changes, but when they exhibit behaviours during seasonal changes we'll need to keep in mind what might be behind these things and do what we can to assist.

That can mean helping them to find fabrics that are less irritating. For some it might mean cutting the tags off, so nothing is rubbing on the backs of their neck or there is no seam across the toe of socks, that might drive the child crazy. For others it might mean gradually introducing the upcoming change.

～

S ome kids actually pay attention better when they are fidgeting with something. Think about adult behavior. Do you know anyone who flicks the end of their ballpoint pen when they're concentrating? Do you know anyone who doodles during meetings? Taps their spoon? Raps her fingers on the table? Many of us do these things and they might be unconscious habits that we've developed in childhood that actually help us be calm or to concentrate.

Decades and decades ago in schools we wanted kids to sit at their desk with their hands nicely folded on the desktop or in their lap. Those days are long gone (and actually I'm not sure that expectation worked for many children). There are kids who are distracted by having something in their hand, so you don't want them to have a fidget, but other kids actually pay attention to the teacher better when they are fidgeting with something in their hand. These are kids who crave tactile stimulation. Their body is under-responsive in this area, meaning that it requires a lot of tactile input for the sensations to register and they need extra tactile input across the day. So, fidgeting with something can be a positive thing.

When I say fidget, I mean something that they can play with or move around in their hands. I do not necessarily mean their most favorite toy in the world because that could be too distracting and take their mind off the task that they should be completing. Stores sell stress balls for adults and if the student has a large enough hand, they can be a good thing. For many kids though, these stress balls are too large for them to wrap their fingers around and get in a good squeeze, so you might need to make your own.

An easy and inexpensive thing to do is to go to a dollar store and buy some balloons. Make sure to get the helium quality balloons which are a little stronger. You might even want to place one balloon inside another just for extra strength. Fill that balloon with something like flour or cornstarch, have the child hold it in the palm of his hand and fill it up just enough so that the child's fingers can squeeze around it comfortably. Then knot the end - actually double knotting would be safer.

Dollar stores are great sources for other fidgets as well. There are balls, there are squishy fidgets, different plastics, different textures and things like that. They will definitely get grubby over time and need to be washed or even replaced but you're only spending a dollar or two each time, so it's not a huge deal.

Another thing to consider from a dollar store is a spool of ribbon. Depending on the child, various sorts of ribbon might appeal to them. You can find ribbon that is smooth and satiny, some that is velvety, some that has more of a texture like corduroy. (For safety's sake, you might want to avoid the ribbon that has thin wires along each side). Each spool is generally only a couple of dollars. Cut off about four inches of ribbon at a time and give it to the child to rub between his fingers and play with. If it's an older kid who doesn't want anyone to know that they are fidgeting with something, it can be stuck in his pocket and the rest of the class need never know. Yes, the ribbon is going to get very grubby, probably pretty quickly, but just throw it out and cut off another four or five inches.

I once knew a boy who had intense tactile cravings. It took quite some time to find out what worked well for him. What we finally settled on had absolutely no appeal to me but really worked for him. It was one of those plastic scrubbing things that you would use when you're doing dishes. When it was cut in quarters, it was about the right size for his hand. If this grade four boy fidgeted with his piece of scrubber in one hand, he could easily get twenty minutes of solid seat work completed independently and accurately. Without that scrubby fidget he would not get five minutes done and even then, would require some adult assistance to do it.

Older students (or adults) might not "outgrow" their need for tactile fidgets. Some will fiddle with their pen; some might gravitate to smoking devices. There is a whole array of fidget rings for males and females. They are stylish and functional. Here[1] is just one example.

~

When upset, we might try to soothe a child with a gentle touch. We feel hurt when that child pulls away from our efforts to comfort him. That tiny wisp of caress on his skin might be akin to nails on a blackboard to a child who is easily over-aroused by tactile sensations. For that child, a firm touch might be far more welcome and soothing. We'll talk more about firm touches and pressure in the chapter on Proprioception.

OLFACTORY SENSORY SYSTEM

Olfactory has to do with your sense of smell. Many kids who are on the autism spectrum are highly sensitive to smells. As a teacher or administrator, I would simply not wear perfume or aftershave. I don't think it's worth it. While you might enjoy your scent, it might be enough to totally put the child off their day.

Some kids can be sensitive to the odor left behind by cleaning products, including surface disinfectants and laundry products. While the television advertisements might extol the virtues of leaving behind scents on your clean laundry, that could be exactly what you do not want to do for an autistic child who has olfactory sensitivities. Some smells in a small amount might be very pleasant but if you ramp that odor up by ten or twenty times, that's how it might feel to highly sensitive child. Think about the chemical residues that might be left behind after the custodial staff have wiped off the student desks. Might a rinse of vinegar and water do the job instead of chemicals that are offensive to a student?

. . .

A s I said before, with any of these sensory areas you can be over sensitive or under sensitive. If you are over sensitive, then even a small amount of input registers on your system. If you are under sensitive, then your body requires a lot more input before it can register.

If the child is under sensitive in say the olfactory area, then they can be described as sensory-seeking. That means that their body is craving stimulation to fill that void. The variety and intensity of smells might be just fine for you but to that child, who needs more before the sensation registers, there is an absence and he is seeking stronger smells. You might see such a child sniffing marking pens or even worse, there are things that are more inappropriate for him to smell.

I know a young guy who really sought out strong odors. He would try to put his nose into the armpits of people, both people he knew and strangers. If someone got up from a chair, he would put his nose where the person had been sitting. He would also put his nose to people's rear ends. As you can imagine, this was going to get him in lots of trouble, especially when he did it to strangers on the street.

Surprise, surprise, telling him no didn't work. Neither did, "Stop that!". And, his parents tried giving him some negative consequences which didn't work either. What did help though, was addressing his sensory need - that craving for more olfactory input. One boy who was having this challenge went with his mom to the store and they tried out all kinds of plug-in air fresheners until they found the one that he liked the best. That was on in his room nonstop. It solved the problem of trying to smell inappropriate things in public but he then was spending most of his time alone in his room. So, the family found a plug-in air freshener of the same scent that was movement-activated and plugged it in the family room. Initially this boy walked by it what felt like a hundred times a day, but he was getting some of the input he needed and was calmer.

Another boy I know who was showing similar behaviors required even more olfactory input. He also liked to draw. His family found some marking pens at an office supply store and these marking pens each had a very distinctive odor - awful odors to the perception of many people, but he loved them. (They include dill pickle, barnyard smells, etc. You can find them here[104]).

He also used nasal inhalers; one that he really liked was a lavender smell. Here [105] is an example. You can get them in a variety of odors now. This child kept one in his pocket and used it quite frequently during the day. The upside was that he no longer tried to put his nose in people's butts or their armpits.

VISUAL SENSORY SYSTEM

⁂

As you likely already divined, the visual sense has to do with the information that you take in with your eyes. Like the other senses, an individual can require more than average input to register the sensation or can be sensitive to even small bits of incoming information. And this level of sensitivity can vary for that person.

Years ago, teachers of young children were taught to make their classrooms bright and colorful. Attention-grabbing objects dangled from the ceiling and the room was awash with bulletin boards, posters and artwork.

The trend in more recent years is to tone this down. It's not only autistic kids who can be over-stimulated and have their attention taken off-course by too much competing stimuli. Many of today's classrooms will have fairly plain walls where the instructor teaches. This means that the children's attention is focused on the speaker or the information that the teacher is portraying on the black board, white board or projector. There might be other very colorful areas of the classroom, but those are spots where the children would be directed for a specific purpose or for those kids who learn best with more intense visual stimulation. You will notice classrooms whose bookshelves are hidden by plain curtains that are only drawn back when the kids are invited to go to those areas. This is part of the term Universal Design for Learning[106]. While UDL encompasses far more than just the visual environment, organizing your classroom space is an important concept in UDL.

If you'd like to learn more about Universal Design for Learning, check out this link[107]. If you prefer to learn through video rather than reading, try here[108]. You can take a free, self-directed learning course on UDL here[109]. And, check out this toolkit [110] for UDL.

Cluttered classrooms can be disorienting to kids who have visual sensitivities. Their eyes might not know where to light and the mass of visual detail coming in could be overwhelming.

Some autistic people are excellent at details, but this can mean that they can't see the forest for the trees. The individual features jump out at them and demand their attention. They find it hard to let all that extraneous detail recede into the background. They can get lost in the chaos of all the visual input coming at them. The teacher can get lost in all this confusion.

This has to do with a term called Central Coherence. With good Central Coherence you automatically know which things in the environment you need to pay attention to. With poorer Central Coherence, everything comes at you with the same intensity and the details pop out just as much as the main features that *you* might attend do. It can take a lot of conscious effort to recognize and catalog all that input and purposely decide to let some things slide off while you focus on other aspects. For most of us this is a totally unconscious act. Imagine the energy it would take to have to concentrate on this all the time. No wonder autistic kids are drained at the end of a school day.

∼

As mentioned in the auditory chapter, our classrooms today are busy places with lots of sound and motion. Even if the noises do not seem to bother a child, the motion might. A child who can ignore auditory distractions might be interrupted by the flash of color as someone walks by their desk.

Some classrooms are lucky enough to have individual study carrels available, a desk with elevated sides along 3 edges. This helps block out some of the visual stimuli in the room. But they are scarce in schools and there are certainly not enough for all the students who would benefit.

It's possible to make improvised study carrels but cutting a cardboard box so that it has 3 sides, without a top or bottom. Try for a box that is relatively the same size across as a child's desk. When the box is not in use, it can be folded flat and placed along a wall. When a child feels that closing off his view of the classroom would help him work better, he could retrieve a box and spread it out along the top of his desk.

I am not a fan of having a strategy available to just one child. Why make him feel different? And, there are many undiagnosed kids in a classroom who would also benefit from certain strategies. If half a dozen such boxes are available for whomever would like to use one that period, why not applaud any child who understands enough about his own learning style to know what this technique would help him?

~

To many of us, lighting does not matter much. Sure, if it's too dark then we turn on a light to better see. But if you are sensitive to lights, then there can be a great difference.

Fluorescent lights flicker. Most people do not notice but someone sensitive would. (These lights also hum, potentially bothering a person who has auditory sensitivities). My preference would be to have no fluorescent lights in the building, but that is not reality. Sometimes ensuring that the ballast is not wearing out will reduce that distracting flicker. But other accommodations might be needed. Some people find that wearing a visor or ball cap deflects some of the flickering from their vision and they are then less distracted. For some, sunglasses might help.

Likely natural light would be best as much as possible. Incandescent, halogen and LED lights are more comfortable for some students. A series of floor lamps might work. Keep in mind that you can often get different hues within a type of bulb. Some larger hardware stores have displays in the lighting section where you can turn various kinds of lighting on and off to see which one feels more soothing. Dimmable lights might also be helpful if that is an option in your school.

~

Tents can be wonderful things. They are cozy and feel safe, plus they are a nice way to block out excess stimulation. Who doesn't enjoy crawling into a tent? You can find small, pop-up tents, appropriate for small children that could duck into the corner of a primary school classroom. Your autistic student will definitely not be the only student seeking the quiet seclusion of that tent, on occasion. A larger tent would provide enough room for several children and some pillows for a cosy reading area, or even enough room for a teacher. You can read about how tents are used for this purpose in the novel, *Autism Goes to School*[111].

And speaking of sleep, were you aware of the warnings about blue light impeding sleep? Blue light is given off by screens. Modern technology has made screen use so easy and so appealing. Even very young children know how to push and swipe and press with their fingers to make a device do what they want it to do. While once televisions were considered babysitters, smart phones, tablets and similar devices are now right up there alongside TVs.

I am NOT anti-technology and rather like techie things myself. I get that when parents come home from work and are trying to prepare supper, having a child amuse himself with a tablet is handy. The American Academy of Pediatrics[112] has a statement recommending limits of screen time for kids.

Apart from the amount of time a child stares at a screen, there is also concern about *when* that child has screen time. Blue light surpasses the body's production of melatonin, a naturally occurring substance that helps us fall asleep. An hour or two before bedtime, restrict screen time. Instead let this be a time for a calming bath, having a snack, reading a story and snuggling. If a parent complains to you about their child's poor sleep patterns, you might consider sharing with them: How Blue Light Affects Kids and Sleep[8].

AUDITORY SENSORY SYSTEM

I once knew a seven-year-old girl who had an autism diagnosis and didn't show a lot of challenging behaviours. But at school as one winter arrived, she seemed to change. This once quiet child began pushing and fighting with other kids and tantrumming. She would fight about putting on her winter clothing and going outside for recess. This was quite different than her previous behaviors.

It took a while of observing to try to figure out what was happening. When she was thrust into her snow pants you could see her face change as she walked down the hall, looking ready to blow. There was this swish, swish, swish as the legs of the material of her snow pants rubbed together. We tried having her go out for recess without those snow pants and there was far less hassle. The sound was bothering this little girl.

I realize that there are millions of kids who have swishy snow pants on in the cold winter and are just fine, but for this one particular child either the pitch or something about that sound just drove her. Her grandma sewed her new snow pants. These were made out of corduroy instead of that water-resistant material and didn't make the same sound at all. When she was given those, the behaviors, including the fighting and the tantrums stopped.

What was bothering her was auditory input. Something about the pitch or the quality of the sound of those swishing snow pants truly irritated her.

Think about sounds that might bother you as an adult. A common one is nails on a blackboard. For me if I listen to music and there is something slightly off key, it really grates on my nerves. Some of us might relish going to a rock concert while others absolutely abhor the volume of sound that would be an onslaught to their ears. For an autistic person with auditory sensitivities, this goes far beyond mere preferences or annoyances and can seem unbearable.

Ever wonder what it might be like to be extremely sensitive to sounds in everyday situations? Take a look at this simulation[113]. Think about your noise-sensitive students who walk to school and what stressors they face before arriving at your door. This video[114] clip will give you an idea of what it might be like for them. Here is a virtual reality experience[115] of an autistic child shopping with his mom in a mall.

～

You will encounter students who have no difficulty hearing and, on a test, their hearing acuity is just fine. Yet, they will have trouble processing the words that they hear. Some students will actually receive a diagnosis of central auditory processing disorder[116]. Try this simulation[117] of what it would be like to pay attention and get directions within a cacophony of classroom noises.

～

There are autistic kids who have incredible hearing. Parents say that they might be talking quietly in another room in the home and their child can hear every word that is said. Teachers say they might be whispering to someone across the classroom and that one student can still hear them.

School classrooms nowadays are not quiet places. That is just the way it is. No longer are kids expected to sit silently throughout the day, but they are encouraged to discuss approaches and problems with one another. They are free to get up out of their seats to go sharpen a pencil, to go get a book, to go ask the teacher a question. There is movement and there is noise.

A few decades ago, many schools had hallways and classrooms that were carpeted. Then there were concerns about mold and allergies and many buildings removed all the carpeting. While possibly easier to clean, the floors that are left are definitely noisier than those classrooms where carpeted flooring absorbed some of the sounds. To a sensitive child this can be overwhelming.

Let's think outside of the classroom as well. There is frequent movement in the hallways outside of the classroom door, whether that door is open or closed. Many schools have metal lockers. And those clang loudly as the doors are opened and closed.

Most schools have some kind of bell or buzzer that signals class change time, when it's time for recess or lunch or to go home and those bells or buzzers can be at a frequency or pitch that some kids find difficult to handle. (Actually, I know some teachers who complain a lot about the type of bell their school uses).

Then, one of the worst sounds is that of the fire alarm. Schools are required to have fire drills and for very good reasons. In most places by law some of those fire drills must be a surprise, not planned. That might mean that only the administrator knows when the alarm is to going blare for a drill and neither the teachers nor the students know. Safety wise, this can certainly make sense so that the kids have practiced over and over what to do and how to vacate the building safely and were to go while you wait outside. But that sudden hugely loud noise can be really difficult for some kids who have auditory sensitivities. This includes many kids who are autistic, but many other kids might also be sensitive to the sounds.

The fire alarm simply has to be loud; there's no way around that. Some schools handle this by breaking the element of surprise. For just the one or two students who might be thrown into a total panic by the unexpected alarm these kids might be pre-warned. I know of one child who even when he knew the alarm was going to ring later that morning was in an absolute frenzy of anxiety before it happened and then had a huge meltdown when it finally sounded. (In fact, his entire morning was a disaster as he anticipated this upcoming, terrifying noise).

The principal made a different plan for the next surprise fire drill. He talked to the child ahead a time and asked for his help. He asked the child if he would please push the buzzer for him when it was time for the next drill. They spend lots of time talking about the purpose of fire drills and how to keep everyone safe and that this was going to be this child's job to help out the school. They drew pictures about it and went over and over a story they made up about fire drills. When the day came the child spent some time with the principal in the office ahead of time then he donned his noise cancelling headphones and with his hand on the principal's, together they pushed the buzzer. Possibly since it was under his control and there had been so much planning ahead of time, there was no meltdown this time.

So, noise cancelling headphones can be a boon for anyone who has auditory sensitivities. We are not going to make our classrooms silent places; it's just not going to happen. For some kids, noise cancelling headphones can help them concentrate much better and to be calmer. Some kids who also have tactile sensitivities might not like the fee of that headphone strap across the top of their head. Those kids might want to wear that strap part against the back of their neck or down under their chin.

You can now get noise cancelling earbuds that will be far less conspicuous than headphones. Some kids keep them in their pocket and just pull them out when they need to quiet things down so that they can work better. Some don't need noise cancelling earbuds just regular earbuds that will dampen down the sound a little bit. For some people listening to music while they work is helpful and not distracting.

If you go to a pharmacy or drugstore there are lots of different kinds of earplugs you can find. The ones that I like are shaped almost like little foam drums that you can squish in place in your year. They definitely do not remove all sounds from the environment, and you can often hear some speech sounds but it is muted enough that it could help some kids from becoming overwhelmed.

∽

I n some classrooms you might notice a teacher wearing a head set, lapel or other type of microphone. This is likely connected to a sound field system. There are many brands, but they serve similar functions. They raise the sound of the teacher's voice above that of the hubbub in the room. That doesn't mean that the teacher's voice is necessarily louder, but it is more obvious, making it easier to pay attention to the teacher's words. His or her voice is carried wirelessly to a central speaker. Some are mounted permanently in the ceiling of the classroom; some are portable and can be carried from room to room. Many are also connected to Smart Boards so that videos, etc. can be played through the speakers. There are personal systems where the teacher's voice is projected to a device that a specific student carries, such as a child with a hearing impairment. My preference is for classroom-wide projection as it benefits so many kids.

Initially, some teachers will be reluctant to use the system and wear a microphone. They are self-conscious about their voice. They worry about remembering to turn it off when the leave the classroom. If they speak to someone in the hall, the staff room or use the washroom, all those sounds will be carried back to the classroom's speakers.

I have never met a teacher who did not cherish their speaker system by the end of the year, even if they were reluctant users initially. They say that they are less fatigued at the end of the day because they did not have to work at projecting their voice. Most report that kids pay better attention. And, most telling is the fact that when a substitute teacher is in the room for the day, the children remind the sub to wear the microphone because they prefer it.

Some lucky schools have a sound field system built into every classroom. More often though, one is ordered with the needs of a particular student in mind. At the end of the year, a built-in system must be taken out and re-installed in that child's next classroom. Teachers are sorry to see them go. While the teachers appreciate them, they are also helpful for kids who have hearing impairments, attentional issues, autism, fetal alcohol syndrome, and those with many other learning differences.

∼

I've talked about the sound environment in schools because school is often a stressful place for autistic kids, but let's move on to our home environments now. There are noises in our living spaces that you are likely not fond of, but don't really think about because they are part of life. Take for instance the vacuum cleaner. It's probably only the rare person who truly enjoys vacuuming but we do it anyway. Think about the sounds - the running motor, the sucking noise, the clatter as bits of dirt move around the brushes and get gobbled up. The decibel level and pitch vary machine to machine, but some might be in that truly irritating range for a particular autistic child.

You're not going to abandon vacuuming, but keep in mind that the sound might contribute to your child's distress. Perhaps don't run the blender right before or after vacuuming if that high-pitched whirl bothers your kid.

I know a child who found it difficult to eat at the table with this family because the sounds of their chewing drove him up the wall. He described them as gooey, smacking, watery sounds and if he looked toward their mouths, he was grossed out by glimpses he could see of masticated food. His preference was to eat alone in his room; his parents wanted him to be with the family at the dinner table. The compromise was that he wore ear buds during supper. (Over time his auditory sensitivities decreased and he was able to eat with others without covering his ears).

One form of auditory input that many parents hate is that of the automatic hand dryers found in many restrooms, even in schools. Some parents say that it's so hard to take their autistic child shopping or to a restaurant because they are terrified of the hand dryer sound. (What is worse - you and the child wiping your wet hands on your clothes or forcing him to use the hand dryer?) Hand sanitizer and wet wipes might become your friend.

∾

In a couple chapters we're going to look at proprioception. Giving your student proprioceptive input is often a good way to make auditory sensitivities easier to handle. It's certainly worth a try.

GUSTATORY SENSE

G ustatory is all about our oral motor area, the mouth. It refers to things around the outside of the mouth, feelings on the inside of the mouth as well as taste. (We cover some of the gustatory challenges in the chapter *What If He Won't Eat At School?*). For now, let's start with the outside of the mouth first.

Despite the fact that most of us learn to have some control over our drool by the time we reach our third birthday, some autistic kids have weak oral motor control and are slower in coming to this. Having saliva dribble from their lips may still be a problem when they are school age. A speech/language pathologist or/and an occupational therapist might be able to give your child exercises to help firm up his muscular control around his mouth to reduce the drooling. Even simple activities such as sipping through a straw can help develop the musculature in the oral region.

If a child is drooling, you might think that you should approach him or her when you see that saliva edging out of the corner of the mouth and down the person's chin, and gently mop it up very lightly and tenderly. But this could have the opposite effect to what you are going for. Your tender ministrations might arouse feelings in him that you did not anticipate. The area around the outside of the mouth and particularly the chin and lower jaw can be sensitive areas for many autistic people and that very light caress on the chin could send willies down the spine of that individual. You know, that nails on the blackboard kind of shutter-inducing feeling? This could cause the student to freeze, to pull away, to be suspicious of the next moves that you might make or even to lash out or try to run away. Rather than that soft, almost-not-there touch swipe his whole chin slowly but firmly if that child has tactile sensitivities, particularly around his mouth. And, it wouldn't hurt to let him know ahead of time what you are going to do and why you are wiping up that drool (that he is likely unaware of).

～

Y ou might notice that your student's teeth appear yellow and coated A dentist might look aghast at the condition of a child's teeth. He might turn to the parents and admonish them on the importance of daily brushing and flossing their child's teeth or the ramifications down the road will not be pretty. While the parent might look guilty and concerned, most likely it's not that they don't know this information. They are aware of how important it is to look after a child's teeth, but this may definitely be easier said than done. You might be in a position to offer the parents of your student some suggestions. They'll appreciate your support rather than your censure.

Let's consider some of the reasons why. The mouth can be a sensitive area, particularly for some autistic children. Often parents of toddlers begin dental care by putting their finger in the child's mouth and brushing the teeth that way, perhaps with some kind of cover over their finger. Or they use a washcloth. As the child's mouth gets a bit bigger, they may progress to using a baby-sized toothbrush.

Is brushing with a cloth or a wet brush enough? Generally, the advice is to use toothpaste. But let's hold off a while before simply putting something into the child's mouth.

For a child with lots of oral sensitivities having something stuck into his mouth can be an unpleasant experience. There are even some toddlers who find the progression from breast-feeding or bottle feeding to having a spoon or fork in their mouth unpleasant. The metallic taste of a spoon can be abhorrent to some so the parents might use plastic. As the parent attempts to insert a toothbrush and rub it around those fledgling teeth the child might be actively squirming, trying to pull their head out of the parents reach and their tongue will be trying to evict that intruder. Some parents get their fingers bitten while they attempt oral hygiene on their child. Having something placed inside their mouth can be almost repulsive to some kids.

Then there is the whole toothpaste issue. You will come across parents who have a problem with their child eating the toothpaste. Some of those pastes are particularly flavored to appeal to children, including bubble-gum lovers. While those strong tastes might appeal to some children, this can be a real issue for autistic kids. Many find strong tastes abhorrent.

You might say that there are many, many toothpastes on the market and surely, the parent can find one that will appeal to their child. That's a logical assumption, but in my experience it does not always hold true. After a certain age, parents might be able to apply the suck-it-up factor and insist that the child simply tolerate that taste for the minute it will take to get the teeth brushed. To most of us that doesn't seem like too much to ask. But, if you are autistic and all day long your body has been assaulted by sensory invasions and you're at the end of your rope and exhausted, having to go through this ritual before bed could just be altogether too much and the child will have a meltdown.

But put yourself in the shoes of that parent. Like the child, you are tired; it's been a long, hard day. You just want to get this child into bed and asleep so you can put your feet up and recharge your batteries before you need to go at it again the next day. Is it worth the fight to brush his teeth? Couldn't we let it go just this one night and will make sure to do it tomorrow night? I can see you nodding your head. Yes, it doesn't seem like the end of the world to skip brushing those teeth one evening, but it's a slippery slope from there.

Say your child has gotten by the horror of having an object in his mouth, and there is one particular kind of toothpaste that doesn't instantly bring on the child's gag reflex. But then as you start brushing the teeth, the toothpaste sort of fluffs up in his mouth. It doesn't remain in that thick cream form, but it alters in his mouth cavity. How would that feel to him? Yes, I know you feel it yourself several times each and every single day. But you don't have autism and sensory sensitivities.

A dentist once told me that if a child has a major aversion to all forms of toothpaste, then just brushing with water is better than nothing. He also had another suggestion. Place some baking soda in the palm of your hand and dip the wet brush into the soda. Then use that to brush his teeth. Again, there's a strong taste involved in that as well as a texture of the gritty substance on the teeth and in the mouth.

The sense of taste can be so particular to some children who have autism that taste and certain textures in the mouth can bring out their gag reflex. There are parents I know for whom it is just the norm that when they brush their child's teeth, they know the child will throw up.

~

Because of the issues around taste and texture many autistic kids are very picky eaters. Getting a well-balanced diet into the child can seem almost impossible. Still having a child throw up their bedtime snack is disheartening when they have put little food into their stomach all day.

Along with taste and texture issues in the mouth there is also the question of temperature. Some kids will only want items that are lukewarm in their mouth and cannot tolerate anything to warm/hot or too cold.

Mealtime is a very sensory event. There are the tastes, textures and temperatures of the foods that we just mentioned. But there is a visual appeal (or the opposite) to the foods on our plates also. There are typical children who do not like their foods to touch each other. Or, they don't want to eat anything green. For an autistic child, multiply this aversive reaction exponentially.

Food smells. Most often we hope that it is a good aroma, but certain smells might be off- putting to an autistic child, either during the cooking stage or when sitting in front of a plate.

Then there are the sounds involved at the dinner table. Although we attempt to never chew with our mouths open, people with sensitive hearing will pick up on those chewing and smacking sounds. Forks scrape against plates, cutlery clatters and chairs squeak. Would your child eat better while wearing headphones? That might be a better alternative to having him eat on his own.

We'll talk about this more in the vestibular chapter, but some kids have weak trunk muscles and holding themselves upright after a while can be quite tiring. You might notice your student slumping across the table or putting his head onto the desk while he eats. Consider how he is sitting and the chair he's on. Can his feet touch the floor? You feel unstable when they don't. Perhaps a stool would help. Experiment with different types of seating for him. We'll talk about this more in the next chapter.

All of these sensory issues can make eating difficult for some autistic kids. Parents often worry that their child has an unbalanced diet, but despite their best efforts, the child self-restricts his eating to just a few foods. Why? Because of some of the sensory things we've talked about already, plus another reason. When you are always on high alert, ready to protect your body from external forces that over-arouse it, you tend to shy away from new things, sticking to the tried and true.

VESTIBULAR SYSTEM

T he vestibular system [1]is located in our inner ear, on the temporal bone, near the ear's cochlea but is not part of our hearing system. It has to do with our sense of balance, movement and letting us know where our body is in space.

Have you ever been on one of those merry-go-round-type rides on the playground? You know the platforms that you run and jump on and then it spins around while you hang onto some poles or handles? Most kids jump off of those feeling delightfully dizzy and stumble around the grass for a bit.

There are some children whose body craves vestibular stimulation who can go around and round, get off such a ride and walk perfectly fine. These are kids who have fairly intense vestibular needs.

Another sign that a child is seeking vestibular input is that he will love to rock or really enjoy swinging and those activities have a calming affect for him. For most people the best type of rocking is a forward and back motion rather than side to side, although there are individual differences. Think about when you were holding a baby in your arms. Our instinct is to rock that child in a direction from their head to their feet.

～

A child with sensory processing difficulties can also have the opposite reaction and be easily overstimulated in the vestibular area. This might be a child who has a poor sense of balance. He is unsteady on his feet. He might be the last one in his age group who learns how to hop on one foot or to skip or to ride a bicycle. Some people with vestibular sensitivities are prone to motion sickness as well.

～

Vestibular is a good sense to stimulate in a classroom. There will be many students, not just those with autism but kids who have learning disabilities, fetal alcohol syndrome, and attentional issues who will benefit from the type of stimulation you receive through your vestibular system.

A simple way to supply some vestibular feedback to the child's body is with an assortment of seating possibilities. Search on your favorite online store for seating cushions. You will find round ones, square ones or wedges that you fill with air. The amount of air you use will depend on what feels good to that child. These cushions fit on the child's chair and allow him to wiggle as he sits. They come in many shapes, sizes and styles, but here is one example[2]. That wiggling provides vestibular stimulation.

If the school is lucky enough to have chairs that are not permanently attached to the desk, then there are far more options available. Sitting on the therapy ball is great for some kids because it allows them to bounce up and down to wiggle back and forth or side to side giving their body the stimulation it is craving. For some kids these types of movement actually help him concentrate better on what the teacher is saying and on doing the work. Therapy balls come in the typical round shape you might be familiar with and some have little legs on them to keep the ball from rolling away. You can buy rings that the therapy ball rests in to help keep it in place plus you can even buy a floor ring with a seat back attached to give more support. Therapy balls also come shaped more like a peanut that you straddle and that is comfortable for some kids. But I would not recommend a child sit on the therapy ball all day long because it is tiring for the trunk and abdominal muscles. You don't want the child to start slumping.

This may sound odd, but there are one legged stools that some kids love. It's just how it sounds. There is one leg down the center of the chair with a wooden or a padded seat. The child can rock back-and-forth on it. There are also two-legged stools that give a similar effect. Some of these one- and two- legged stools have the legs adjustable so it will suit various sizes of kids.

Another type of stool is often made of tough plastic, but the bottom is not flat it's slightly rounded and, in a mushroom-looking shape. The round bottom allows it to rock back-and-forth. One brand is called Hokki[3]. (It's available at many online retailers). There are one-legged stools such as this[4] and T-stools such as this[5].

With any of these stools make sure that the child can touch the ground easily. If his knees are not bent at close to a 90° angle, then strain could be put on his lower back.

You can buy child-sized rocking chairs that have stoppers on the front and back legs so that a child cannot over rock and tumble himself and the chair over him. Any classroom I've seen that has such rocking chairs fines that they are in high demand.

As I have mentioned before, I am certainly not a fan of such tools being available only to the autistic child in the classroom. I would rather see several sets of all of these tools available to any child.

~

Who said that we have to be sitting down to learn? I've been in some enlightened classrooms that along the walls are a ledge about elbow high for the kids in that room. Students are free to take their book to that ledge and stand while they do their work. Some lucky classrooms have standing desks. A standing desk is exactly how it sounds. They often have adjustable legs so you can vary the height based on the size of the child. When the child bends his elbow at roughly a ninety degree angle, he should be able to rest the side of his hand on the desktop if it is about the right height for him. Some of the standing desks have a wire between the front or back legs that you can put your foot on and wiggle your foot back-and-forth. This added motion can be helpful. In case you've never seen one, take a look at this one[6]. Other kids might like to stand on one of those seating cushions that I mentioned earlier. That will allow them to wiggle around. Some of these cushions even have what feels like ball bearings inside them to give greater feedback to your body.

Something useful is a swing. Ideally one outdoors and one available inside as well. The vestibular motion of swinging can have a very calming effect.

Another thing I recommend is a tent for young students. Think of those rainy days of your own childhood when you would take a sheet and drape it over a table to make a tent for yourself. Didn't it feel great to be cocooned inside there? You can get small, child size tents, even pop-up types that you can put in a corner of a room. When your student starts to feel overwhelmed, crawling inside a tent can block out some of that excess stimulation and help him to calm down. Having several small tents so that several children can access them, or a larger tent that would fit a group of students (or maybe a teacher plus a couple kids). A third object that can be good for calming is a beanbag chair. Especially an adult-sized one will fold around the child, giving a sense of pressure.

That brings us to the next section, proprioception.

1[19] Vestibular system https://www.neuroscientifical lychallenged.com/blog/know-your-brain-vestibular-system.

[120] Cushion for wobbling https://amzn.to/2YyScN1.

[121] Hokki stool https://amzn.to/2Kq2eap.

[122] One-legged stool https://amzn.to/2KFcZVh.

[123] T-stool https://amzn.to/2YR8bWL.

[124] Standing desk https://amzn.to/2YGJzA5.

PROPRIOCEPTIVE SENSE

N ow we are going to explore proprioception[119,] and this
sense gives a big win for those of you who work or live
with autistic kids.

Place the palms of your hands flat on a table in front of you or
if you're not at a table put them on your knees. Now lean forward
so that you are pressing your weight into your palms. Think about
how that feels. The reason you can feel that pressure is because of
something called proprioceptors. Proprioceptors are nerve
bundles in the large muscles of your body. They help register body
motions and the feeling of weight or pressure. And this is good
news.

The reason why it is good news is that proprioception, weight
and/or pressure, are ways that you can combat the other senses
when they are being overwhelmed or over-aroused. Weight and
pressure may have a calming effect.

And, I say *may* have a calming effect because no one strategy
will ever work for every single person. What I'm saying will apply
to many people and is worth trying. How do you know if it will
work? Well if the person is old enough, ask them. Or ask their

parent or caregiver. Or, try it and see if it has a calming effect. The child's reactions will let you know.

On occasion, you might see a child wearing an unusual vest. They are sometimes made of what looks like padded neoprene or sometimes they are cloth with pockets in them and those pockets contain different size packages of weights. The latter is a weighted vest. Sometimes the weights are applied across the chest and upper back. More often, they are in pockets near the lower edge of the vest. The vest I described is one example of a pressure vest. They can often be snugged up with Velcro or some other type of fastener so that the vest will hug the person closely, giving a feeling of pressure. Here[120] is just one type. Again, weight and pressure can have a calming effect.

Some other examples of weight that you might see are ankle or wrist weights that people might wear when they are exercising. Sometimes these weights are not strapped around the person's ankle or wrist but instead they might be draped over the shoulders, or draped across the lap

With younger children you might see them with a lap weight. [3] It might be a rectangle or round piece cloth stuffed with some heavy weighted material that they put on their lap. Some of the purchased ones are in the shape of a turtle or some other stuffed animal. There are also weights and snakes that are kind of a long thick rope-type piece of fabric that is stuffed with weighted material and the child might have it draped across the back of their neck and down the chest or it might be across their thighs. These are all examples of weighted products that might help make a child feel calmer. Or, an adult for that matter.

If a small child is upset, we might gently rub their hand or their shoulder to help calm them. If you are thinking about the powers of proprioception as a calming strategy perhaps do not stroke that child's hand gently, especially if he has tactile sensitivities. That soft touch could be unpleasant and over-arousing, the opposite of your goal. Instead, firmly hold or press down with more force on their shoulders. You might want to refer back to the chapter where we talked about tactile sensitivities for more cautions about gently rubbing anyone before knowing that they would welcome such a touch.

❧

Heavy work activities provide a sense of pressure and engage the proprioceptors. Your house offers many opportunities to use those large muscle groups, from wall push-ups to wheelbarrow races to doing the vacuuming. Here are fifty heavy work activities for kids[4].

Pushing and pulling are good proprioceptive activities. TheraBand and TheraTubing are useful for this. You can find them at exercise fitness shops and online retailers. They come in different strengths (levels of resistance); generally, the color designates the strength.

Is your student forever kicking the seat of the child in front of him? If some of the seating cushions we mentioned in the vestibular chapter don't help, consider tying some TheraBand[5] around the legs of his chair. He can press on the stretchy band with his feet, giving his body needed proprioceptive input and perhaps allowing you to have a more peaceful classroom

When a child is in the throes of a meltdown after being overwhelmed, the odds are slim that you can get through to him to do some heavy work activities. That is the time to just wait. Let him know that you're there if he needs you but keep your talking to a minimum and give his body time to wind down. Instead, think of heavy work as preventative measures. A healthy dose of regular heavy work will help, as will doing such activities at those earliest signs that the child might be getting over- aroused.

While it is great if you can get to recognize those signs, it will be even better if your student can gradually come to recognize those signs and take action on his own. Isn't that your goal? After all, you cannot always attend to that student and you want him to be able to develop the skills so that he can self-regulate.

In the previous chapter I mentioned three items I find useful - a tent, a swing and a bean bag chair. The latter provides the body with proprioceptive feedback, especially if a child sits in an adult-sized one. The chair will fold around him and accommodate his movements, while giving him the feeling of pressure. Some kids like to place the bean bag chair on top of them, giving them the feeling of weight, as well as pressure.

A bean bag chair could be especially helpful if you coupled that with a weighted blanket[6]. Weighted blankets even bring comfort to people who don't have an autism diagnosis. If you try a weighted blanket your child will quickly let you know if it does not suit him. If not, don't push it.

Weighted blankets are available at specialty shops, many online retailers or you can make your own. A quick search on Pinterest, You Tube or a search engine will show you lots of ways you can sew one yourself. The same holds true for weighted vests and pressure vests. If you make or buy a weighted product, you might wonder how heavy it should be. That would depend on the size of the child. While it might be tempting to put a twenty-pound weight on a hyperactive five-year-old, restrain yourself. The rule of thumb generally is that the weight should be about five to ten percent of the child's body weight. This is just a rough guess though and you'll need to experiment. Some vests come with pockets able to hold an assortment of weights, so you have some options. Here is some information on weighted products[7] that might help.

A common question is how long a weighted vest or other product should be left on. I have found no definitive answer to this. Some specialists say that after twenty minutes or so the body becomes used to that degree of weight and it is no longer doing its job. Remove the vest for an hour, hour and a half then you could try it again.

~

A word about weighted vests and this is just a pet peeve of mine. Don't put something on the child that makes him look dorky. Little kids might not notice nor care. And some older kids might not notice either, but their peers will. You can purchase weighted vests[8] that are stylish - often denim vests not unlike that which their peers might don. Some look like hoodies.

There are also pressure vests. While they have no weights, they will give the feeling of pressure which works well for some kids. Some of these pressure vests have an air nozzle allowing the child to increase or decrease the amount of air in the vest, altering the amount of pressure he feels. These are discrete and no one need know that he is not wearing an ordinary vest or hoodie. Some vests[9] combine both weight and pressure.

Back in the 1940s and 50s fur coats were popular. Ever seen those big, heavy things? I once scoured every second-hand shop I could find to pick up these coats. They weigh a ton and many kids loved them. Sitting on a bean bag chair, a fur coat draped over them and a hand stroking the fur helped soothe many kids.

I know a boy who relished the feeling of pressure on his feet. He would tie his high-top sneakers tightly, saying that they made him feel good that way.

Spandex biker shorts and tank or t-shirts can also give the feeling of pressure. A tight tank top can help some kids tolerate the feel of a loose, floppy sweat shirt.

~

H ere is the really neat thing about weight and pressure - it can help counteract the effect of the other senses when someone is getting overwhelmed. Wearing a weighted vest into a gymnasium may help some kids tolerate the noise of that large, echoey space. A compression garment giving the feeling of pressure can help some kids tolerate the sounds, smells and distractions of their environment. Unlike with weights, there is not the concern about how long a pressure garment can be worn.

Think about those out-of-routine things that happen at school Would it help if your student had access to a weighted blanket and a quiet place to sit when he needed to regroup or calm down? Might he be able to stand the noise and confusion better if he wore some type of weighted or compression garment? Would it hurt to try?

A t school, gyms are often the hardest place for kids who are autistic and have sensory sensitivities. One boy told me that he felt dizzy when he entered the gym - the ceiling seemed so high, like it went on forever and he could get lost or float away.

If the child has olfactory sensitivities, gymnasiums smell (especially after the high school boy's teams have been practicing in there). Visually, things are different in the gym. Apart from that high ceiling, the walls are farther apart, there are bright, colored lines drawn on the floor and the lighting might differ from that in the rest of the building.

For a child with auditory sensitivities, the gym can be a nightmare. Sounds echo. Squealing voices come from all around. There's the thunk of bouncing balls, the slap of ropes smacking the floor and all manner of noises, depending on the activities.

Often when a classroom of kids enters a gymnasium the instructions are to run laps. This is a good warm-up activity but consider it from a sensory view. Many autistic kids have difficulty with gross motor activities and may not be as coordinated as their peers as they run in circles around the room. If he has vestibular issues, his sense of balance may be weak. To counteract this, he might spread his legs in a wider stance and hold his arms out to the side. As he moves, he might pound his feet into the floor, trying to give himself proprioceptive feedback to help ground himself.

AUTISM QUESTIONS TEACHERS ASK

If he has tactile sensitivities, he'll worry that some other child might brush his arm as they run past. He might hug the wall, brushing the edges with his fingertips.

(Unfortunately, he might accidentally rip some of the posters dotting that wall, but that was not his intention.)

His visual sensitivities make all the colorful clothing race by him in a blur, making it difficult to pick out the individual children, in turn making it all that much harder to dodge them so that his arm won't get brushed.

While he is struggling with all this, many of his classmates are having a great time. Their high-pitched giggles fill the air. Their sneakers make sharp squeaking noises irregularly on the floor. There is the persistent slap, slap of their many feet.

Can't you just feel the pressure building inside this child? He's trying his best to hang on, but it's becoming all too much and then what does the teacher do? She blows this piercing whistle and it's all too much and the child has a meltdown.

He's sent out of the gym (thank goodness, he feels). The teachers say that the upset came out of the blue - no one was touching him, and nothing happened. Well, from the outside, it might seem that way, but the assault on this child's senses was tremendous. Sure, last week he tolerated it, but that was different. Today his family woke up late and had to scurry around to make it out of the house on time. He couldn't find his favorite shirt and the sock he put on had a hole in it, making his big toe poke through and you know how much that bugs him. In the morning rush he forgot his homework on the kitchen table beside his bowl of dry cereal because they'd run out of milk.

Any one, two or even three of these things might have been tolerable on a good day but the tsunami of little things built and built until it was all too much to handle. No, the meltdown did not come out of nowhere.

I am in no way suggesting that autistic children should not take part in gym class. They certainly should. The exercise is great, and it is part of the curriculum, but they might require some accommodations and understanding.

Perhaps he could do an alternate warm-up activity, one in a quiet corner of the room. Perhaps he could be in charge of lugging out the gym mats or the ball containers and set things up for the lesson. He could run a timer or counter, checking the number of laps the kids run. While the others do their warm-up run, this might be a good time for someone to go over a social story with the child, letting him know what will happen during gym period.

Think about pressure and weight. Would the gymnasium be more tolerable if he wore a weighted vest? A compression vest? Ankle weights under his pants where no one would see them? None of these are difficult accommodations to make and could make a big difference to the child.

Anxiety

Anxiety[10] seems to plague many autistic people. In fact, anxiety seems on the rise in the general population.

For autistics, the anxiety might be exacerbated by a couple things - sensory challenges and social communication difficulties. If you are always on guard, trying to protect yourself from possible sensory onslaught, you would be anxious. Our lives are full of social situations. If you have the feeling that things in the social realm are going over your head, that you don't quite get what seems to come naturally to others, your anxiety could increase.

Proprioception techniques can be your friend. Keep in mind that weight and/or pressure can have a calming effect and use this in anxiety-producing situations.

INTEROCEPTIVE SENSE

I nteroception[119] is often the most difficult sense to understand. For most of us, interoceptive skills are things we have never thought about. Interoception has to do with the ability to read our body's internal states. Our bodies give us lots of signals - they tell us when we're hungry, thirsty, tired, cold or hot, need to void our bladder or bowels, when something hurts, etc.

Our bodies have sensors throughout them. These sensors gather information and send it to our brains to let us know about our physical state.

Some autistic kids are slow to take to toilet training. Weak interoception might have something to do with this - they have decreased ability to recognize the sensations that tell them when they need to go.

Parents might tell you how tough their autistic child, with a high pain tolerance. Maybe. But it might be that those sensations of discomfort don't easily penetrate the child's awareness or if they do he is unable to pinpoint the source of his feeling of malaise.

Self-regulation is a collection of skills we badly want our autistic kids to acquire. But regulating your emotional state has a lot to do with interoception.

We want our kids to be able to calm themselves. But to calm yourself you need to be able to recognize that you are upset. We know we're upset because of various body feelings - our heart might be racing, our breathing might be quick and shallow, our palms might be sweaty, our shoulders hunched and our fists clenched. That's a lot of body awareness requirements. Self-regulation might come slowly to some autistic kids, because their interoception skills can also be delayed.

Sensory issues affect many autistic children (and adults). We'd like our kids to be able to recognize when things are getting to them, when they are becoming over-aroused. Without adequate interoception, it is difficult to recognize the signs that tell us when we are entering into those states.

This does not mean that your autistic student will always struggle with interoception, or at least to this degree. As he grows and matures, so will this sensory system and he'll become more adept at recognizing his bodily states, especially with guidance.

In the meantime, you can help by reflecting back to him what you observe. He may not be aware that you can tell he is angry because of his clenched fists, raised shoulders, rapid, shallow breathing and his red face. Show him in the mirror what you see and describe how this differs from his resting state. Take pictures to show him how he appears at different times.

When he is calm, have him join you in front of a mirror. Practice trying to make irritated or mad faces. Match your body posture to those emotions. Together, lower your hunched shoulders. Un-fist your hands, shaking out the tension in your arms. Control your breathing with a steady breath in, hold it for a few seconds then release it through your mouth.

Many of the fitness step trackers also measure heart rate. This kind of feedback might help your student learn to recognize when he is over-aroused and signal him to practice some breathing exercises or relaxation techniques to lower his respiration and heartbeat back down to a calmer level.

While some adults find Tai Chi relaxing, the pace frustrates others. It's the same with breathing exercises and you'll need to experiment to learn what works for the student you're working with. Here are a couple examples of ways you might demonstrate and practice with him:

- 8 Fun Breathing Exercises for Kids [131]
- 3 Breathing Exercises to Calm Kids of All Ages[132]

Just like with the other sensory areas, it is possible for a child to be over-sensitive in the interoception area, although this is less common. The incoming information from his body might feel like too much. So, in order to avoid the unpleasant sensation of being hungry, a child might eat constantly so that he doesn't have to experience that pesky feeling. Here is a video[133] that might help you gain a better understanding of this.

Interoception is sometimes called the eighth sense. It is only more recently known and you might have more difficulty finding information on it compared to the other senses. If you're interested in learning more about interoception, consider these sources:

- Autism and the One Big Thing No One is Talking about - Interoception[134].
- Interoception, Neuroscience and Behavior[135].
- How I Feel - Making Sense of Emotions Through Interoception[136]
- Interoception: The "Hidden Sense" [137].

BUT I TEACH HIGH SCHOOL. HOW DOES THIS APPLY TO ME?

❧

"I am a high school teacher. I teach content and I spent a lot of years at university learning this stuff. My students get credit for this class and they take standardized tests. The semester end rolls around quickly and I barely have time to cover all that is in the required curriculum".

Can you relate?

I understand. And, there is a lot of pressure on high school teachers to push your students through the required content. No one could argue with that.

Of the two dozen or so students sitting in your room each day, perhaps a third will readily learn in the way that you prefer to teach (and the way that you, yourself were taught). You might be able to drag another third along with you. But there will always be those students don't seem to grasp the material as readily as you would like.

Not surprisingly, it is the latter third who might worry you the most. They might be the kids who pay less attention or are more unruly, challenging your classroom management skills. Among those might be a student who has a diagnosis of autism.

Although there is no one rule that will fit all students, many autistic kids will take in information that they see much more easily than that which they hear. Many are visual learners.

In the younger grades, visual learners might shine. Kindergarten is a very hands-on year. Even during the primary grades there are still a lot of tactile activities where the kids use manipulatives and other hands-on experiences to learn. Rightly or wrongly, as kids progress through the grades, we tend to offer far fewer hands-on experiences and we switch to talking mode.

From a teacher's point of view, lecturing is one of the most efficient methods of getting information across. It's fast and you can get through what you want to say. If only that was the way that most students learn best, it would be an excellent match. Sadly, that is not the case. And, that might be particularly true when your student has a diagnosis of autism.

A term called central coherence might account for one of the reasons. Central coherence is the ability to pick out of the environment the thing that you most need to pay attention to. For most of us that skill is automatic, and we don't give it a second thought.

Think about the typical classroom. They are not silent places. No matter how excellent your classroom management skills might be, our rooms are no longer silent places. Decades ago, students might be expected to sit at their desk with their hands folded, feet flat on the floor and not utter a sound unless their hand is raised, and the teacher calls on them. For better or worse, those days are gone.

Now, students are freer to move around. One might leave his desk to go sharpen a pencil; another might move around to get a book.

Students are encouraged to talk with one another, to help

problem solve and to discuss. There are definite benefits to this, but one negative is the increased noise level in the classroom.

E ven apart from student movement and student conversations, think about the physical environment of your room. There might be the hum of a fan or a furnace or the air conditioning unit. Many schools are built with fluorescent lights in the ceiling. Although you might not notice it, fluorescent lights hum, especially if the ballast is aging. There is the sound of shuffling feet, the creak of a chair as a student shifts into a more comfortable position. If you truly have enhanced hearing, as do many autistic kids, you will be able to hear the scratch a pencil makes as it moves across a paper.

Those same fluorescent lights that give off a hum will also flicker. Again, most of us will never notice, but a person with visual sensitivity will. If you are lucky enough to have a classroom with windows, sunbeams might come in and dust motes dance in the air. Easy for you to ignore or not even notice, but not if you have autism. That same sun can put a sheen on the blackboard or whiteboard. Some of our student desks have highly polished surfaces that also reflect light from the sun or from the overhead lighting.

While you are teaching, a small part of your subconscious might register the click or hum when the fan starts up. But your conscious brain does not pay it any attention. That is because you have good central coherence.

But if you were autistic, all of these sights, sounds and feelings come at you with the same intensity. Think how easy it would be to feel bombarded if your autistic students must use his conscious brain to decide which obviously plans to ignore. You hope that through all of this, his brain will decide that your voice is the most important thing in the environment.

. . .

The other skill that comes naturally to those with good central coherence is the ability to jump to the salient points, not getting lost in the details. Most autistic people are excellent at noting those little details, but struggle more to see the bigger picture.

If you have not yet done so, read through the chapters on <u>sensory</u> sensitivities to learn more about how your student might be impacted in your classroom.

Despite all this, you still have an obligation to teach the required curriculum. That is a given.

~

How much attention do you pay to the curriculum? I don't mean that in an insulting way at all. But I know that when we get busy and when the pressure is really on, we fall back on what we did last year and the year before and the year before that. It is simply too time-consuming to develop new teaching units all the time.

This can lead to us paying more attention to *our units* than to the actual curriculum. Remember that summer when you spent a whole week devising that wonderful unit on volcanoes? It was a masterpiece and you were justifiably proud. And that first time you taught it, the kids were so engaged and did well.

Curriculums change. Standards, outcomes and indicators are revised. Do your favourite teaching units still align with the current curriculum? Sometimes yes, but sometimes the answer might be no. That can make your heart sink after all the time and energy you put into devising that unit.

Sometimes we get hung up on a student completing our assignment. You definitely need the kids to complete a body of work. Take a look at your assignment and look also at the curricular objectives. Do they line up? You might have asked the kids to demonstrate their knowledge in a certain way, but the curriculum might not stipulate that it must be done in the particular fashion that you stipulated. Is the important thing that the students complete the assignment in the way that you have laid out? Or is the key factor that they demonstrate their knowledge of that concept?

Grade one teachers gather assessments in many different manners. They might ask a child to hand in their written work. They might listen to a child read. They might have him verbally explain how he would tackle an arithmetic problem. They might observe his participation in a group.

As we go higher through the grades, we tend to rely more and more on written tests for our assessments. In some ways this is efficient for some students. But it might not be the best way for all your students to share with you what they have learned.

There will definitely be students in your room who know far more than they are able to put on paper, or that they have time to put on paper. Especially when lengthy answers are required, there are students whose fine motor control issues surface. For them, holding a pen or pencil in a tight grip for a time will be very difficult as their hand and arm will quickly tire. This might make the student shorten his answers as much as possible.

D o you ever wake up some days and feel like your brain is in sluggish mode? It's hard to get all those cylinders firing properly, even after your first cup of coffee. We all have some variations of that from time to time, but this seems to be exacerbated for students who have autism and some other diagnoses. There will be days or times during a day when that student can operate right on, and other days where it is more difficult to get his thoughts together.

Think of all the steps involved in writing a test. First is the requirement of reading. The student must read that question, not only decoding the words but comprehending what those words mean when strung together. For students who have difficulty with either decoding, or comprehension, or both, this could mean reading that question over many, many times. And, the longer the question is, the more difficult the comprehension task will be for your student.

There are a couple things you could do here. You could read the test out loud to your kids before they begin writing it. This might help those who take in what they hear more easily than that which they read.

When you create the test, use short sentences. Don't use a big word when a small one will do. This is not the time to show off your extensive vocabulary. But, in the content area there are times when you must use specific terminology.

Prior to the test, make sure you go over the subject-specific terminology, not assuming that students would have picked up the meaning of that term from the context in which it was used.

On the test, underline or put those terms in bold lettering – something to make them stand out. (You're not trying to trick the kids or even judge their reading ability. You want to know what they have learned in your class).

Rather than writing the question as one long paragraph, break it up into portions, leaving white space around each paragraph. This will make the reading task less onerous. Bulleted points can help as well.

D oes the student have to write his answer in full sentences? If this is a particular part of the English curriculum, possibly yes, but likely not all of the time.

What if the student can tell you the key points of the battle of 1812 using bulleted points? From a teaching point of view, it might make the answers even easier to mark.

You certainly cannot make every test consist only of fill in the blank, true/false or multiple-choice questions. Sometimes a longer explanation is required.

There are kids who might have a lot of information stored in their head that they struggle to put down on paper. If some of those kids could have a conversation with you, they might be able to tell you far more about the topic.

But as it is, it is hard to cram everything into a brief school day. You likely do not have the time to sit with many of your students and have them tell you what they know. Although this is not a bad strategy to use every once in a while, with some kids.

Technology can be a wonderful thing. There are also sorts of options now to record your thoughts. You can buy a standalone audio recorders for maybe fifty dollars. But you need not get that fancy. Most computers have recording options and voice recognition features. Almost all smart phones have some form of voice recognition and the ability to record audio. The same is true of tablets.

There was a time when we felt the need to purchase expensive computer programs like Dragon Naturally Speaking™. That is an excellent piece of software, but it is pricey. Newer iPhones based their voice recognition features on Dragon. Here's an article on the Assistive Technology That's Built into Mobile Devices[138].

Could those students who might be better able to say what they know rather than writing it down, be allowed to use some form of recording or voice recognition software? They could speak their answers aloud and then email that file to you. (This chapter of this book was written in just this fashion).

It is not always easy to find a quiet place in a school where students could do this. But a corner in the library, the very end of the hallway, in between two sets of doors etc. might work.

. . .

Have you heard of curriculum compacting? That is where several subject teachers might get together and pour over their curricula. You might be surprised at the similarities you will find. Some of the English curricular outcomes might be met through the written or oral parts of a history class, for instance. If a student can demonstrate his ability to write an essay for history class, why could he not get credit for demonstrating that skill for his English curriculum as well?

～

Another area that is often a struggle for high school students is taking notes. By now, many students are able to listen to your lecture, pick out the most salient points and write them down while paying attention to what you're saying.

There are many skills involved in doing this. In other chapters we've talked about auditory processing difficulties. While a student's hearing acuity might be just fine, his ability to make sense of your words could be weak. He might require more time, but while puzzling out one statement, you've already moved on to utter several more. Thus, he'd only be picking up part of what you say. Out of every sentence you speak, not every word is key, nor even every phrase. The students must understand what you say and pick out the most important parts. Then they distill these parts into the words that they must write in their notebooks. Most people taking notes do not attempt to scribe every word. Although you likely honed this skill while at university, your students may not be as talented and those with processing difficulties assuredly aren't. Think of all the simultaneous processing this requires - listening, making sense of the words, holding those concepts in your mind, relating them to previously learned material, turning these thoughts into words, then writing down, all the while attending to the next part of your lecture.

There may be times where you write notes on the board and the students are instructed to copy them into their notebooks. This may seem a simpler task but will still pose difficulties for some students. Those with visual sensitivities will find all sorts of things to snag their attention as they move their gaze from their desk to the board. Students with short-term memory difficulties will often write down one word at a time. This is inefficient and involves their eyes scanning to find where they left off after copying each, individual word. Chunking words into phrases or sentences works better but requires an intact working memory.

Students who have fine motor coordination weaknesses who will find holding a pen long enough to write the notes difficult. Students with weak visual perception may have difficulty writing legible notes that begin at the left-hand margin and continue on a straight line to the end of that line, then beginning again on the line directly below the previous one. This is especially true of autistic students whose brain may have difficulty directing its arms and legs into coordinated movements. (Watch Amanda Bagg's video on How to Boil Water[139]).

There are strategies that can make all of this easier, though. Technology might be your student's friend. There are apps to assist as well as smart pens. Smart pens are devices that will make an audio recording of your lecture that can be played back later as an MP3 for studying or translated into text for written review. Here's an example of a LiveScribe pen[140], just one example of the smart pens that are available. Here's a brief video[141] about how it works.

Here are a couple links that might help you assist your students with such tasks:

- 5 Simple Strategies for Note-taking[142].
- 11 Apps to Help Kids with Note-Taking Issues[143]

❧

I s your autistic student on an individualized education plan where he is not following the standard curriculum? There are many sound reasons for inclusion. Working closely with the learning specialist or special education teacher in your building will help you tailor activities that will meet his needs. Here is a nice website with Special Education Resources for Secondary Teachers[144].

W hy is your student who has autism in your classroom? Is he following an academic program and will meet the regular curriculum standards? If so, think about the influences and challenges he has within your room. Consider the fact that he is likely working two or three times harder than are your neurotypical students. Think about how with the sensory influences, the multitasking, and the central coherence challenges it will be exhausting for him. Think about that when you are assigning homework. If you assigned the kids 30 questions are all 30 absolutely necessary? What if he could demonstrate that he has the hang of it by doing half of those questions?

Are there other ways that he (and other students) could demonstrate their knowledge apart from written work? Take a look at the work done by Howard Gardner and his theories of multiple intelligence[145]. Whether or not there is a scientific basis for his theories, his work gives some sound suggestions for alternate ways that kids can show what they know. And, mixing it up with some of these alternate ways tends to engage more of your students. If you do an internet search for "multiple intelligence" plus your subject matter, you'll find a wealth of ideas to tailor to your needs.

WHAT ABOUT WHEN UNEXPECTED THINGS HAPPEN?

⧉

You are quite right to think about this because unexpected things do happen all the time. No matter how conscientiously you have planned out your day something will slip in to interrupt, even if it's something small.

What might be small to you and to many students who can easily let things roll off their backs, might seem like a huge deal to a student who has autism. In fact, people often say that autistic kids tend to make a mountain out of a mole hill, blowing things out of proportion. (If you use that idiom - making a mountain out of a molehill - with your autistic student, they may not get it. Many kids with autism are concrete thinkers and take phrases literally. To help explain this idiom, you could use a video [1]such as this: https://youtu.be/OCxgd1OqcYI)[146].

Getting a handle on the size of the problem seems quite challenging for many autistic kids (and for other students who have difficulties with self-regulation). They seem to have difficulty matching their reaction to the seriousness of the problem. We sometimes talk about kids who "catastrophize[147]", yet to them, the problem can seem insurmountable.

It can seem inexplicable to us when some kids react way out of proportion to what is actually going on. Let's look at an example.

Say the child breaks the lead of his pencil. This is an everyday occurrence that is easily remedied.

But your student throws his pencil and his book to the ground. He begins hollering and wailing. (This might seem an extreme example, but it happens). Here are some of the things that might be running through his mind:

H e only has so much time to complete this assignment and now with this added problem, he might not finish before the bell rings

- He will be in trouble for not finishing on time
- Unfinished work must be done for homework and he hates homework
- When he gets home, his parents will be on his case about not finishing his work at school
- He won't be able to relax on his computer at home before his homework is done
- This was the last pencil in his case, and he doesn't know where to find a replacement
- His weak executive functioning skills mean that organization is a problem for him, so he has trouble finding his pencils
- He has a hard time with activation, and it takes him longer to get down to work, so he is already under time pressure to complete this task
- Anytime his attention is pulled off task, he knows it takes him a long time to return to where he left off
- Executive functioning and narrow thinking make it difficult for him to brainstorm solutions to this problem
- To sharpen his pencil means leaving his desk and walking past other students. They might say something to him or brush against him, sending his tactile defensiveness soaring

- The sound of the pencil sharpener's mechanism grinding on the wood and lead sounds like a jack hammer to his heightened auditory senses, so he avoids it
- This is the last straw. He woke up late only to find that his favorite shirts, (ones that are not scratchy) was still in the laundry hamper, so he had to wear one that itches the back of his neck and his wrists. His sister grabbed his favorite bowl and used it for her cereal. His sock has developed a hole, so the tip of his little toe is poking through, rubbing painfully against the side of his sneaker. The school bus ride was so noisy and so stinky that he hugged his book bag to his chest and rocked the whole time, trying to calm himself. Other kids laughed at him, but all he could think about was trying not to blow up. And, well, you get the idea. The broken pencil might have been just the stick that caused his carefully built, precarious dam to burst.

S o yes, he reacts seemingly out of proportion to what is happening now.

It need not always be that way, though; there are things we can do to assist him in tailoring his response to what is actually happening.

Here's a short video clip[4] that will give a handle on ways to help your students. Here is a poster [5]that will help your students determine just how serious a problem is and how much of an impact it might have.

∾

E ven teachers, with all their great wisdom and experience, can get annoyed when unexpected things happen. Although you have your day meticulously planned, the principal calls an assembly, without warning. Sigh. You know how that will throw off the carefully planned science unit. You know that it's going to mean a loss of classroom time far greater than the forty-five minutes you are sitting in the gym. It takes far longer than most people would think to get the students lined up, travel to the assembly, get seated, experience the agenda, form lines and walk back to the classroom, get seated then back down to work.

As an adult, you know that these things happen and that you'll just have to make up for the time in some way. You always do.

But there are some students in your room who rely on their routine and schedule you have set. This assembly was not on the visual schedule, nor did you even tell the kids about it. Your autistic student might not want to go. It says right there on the schedule that eleven o'clock is math time and now you're trying to make him leave his math work behind and go to the gym. He hates the gym; it smells funny. He hates assemblies because he and his classmates sit on the floor. Someone always brushes their arm against him or knocks his leg with their toe. He hates to be touched. Having the whole school population in the gym at one time creates a bedlam amount of noise and he has to cover his ears, or he can't stand it. The administrator uses the microphone but walks around with it. Every time he nears one of the speakers, the mike gives off this horrendous squeal that is painful on the ears. And, this is *supposed* to be math period. How will he get his work done now? Will he be in trouble for not finishing? Will it be assigned for homework?

Another unexpected occurrence in school is a fire drill. We talk in more detail about that in the auditory chapter.

As carefully as you plan, there will always be things that are out of your control. Isn't that just like life?

You have worked hard to build routines that your students can count on. Now, rather than asking you what comes next, they automatically check the schedule to find that answer and (hopefully) to find which materials they should get ready. They know what to do when they've finished their work. All these routines make your class run more smoothly. Great!

For those kids who have trouble making sense of the world and cling to the established routines, what you've done is a good thing. But it is possible to adhere to routines too rigidly. The deal is that you must establish and teach routines. "We always do it this way, etc." Then, you must teach change.

Even though the schedule clearly states that math is coming up next, make a switch. Pick something that your student normally enjoys, let's say music. Let that student know that there is going to be a change. Be calm, brief and firm, providing visual as well as oral information. Demonstrate to the whole class as you cover the Math sign on the schedule with one that says Music. Explain that the change is just for today. Make that music lesson short and fun. Point out to your student the smiles on the faces of those close to him, and how you can tell that they are enjoying the music.

~

Prep as you will, you cannot prevent unexpected things from happening and they might well upset some of your students. What you *can* do is have your days run as smoothly and predictably as possible, according to the schedule that your students easily access. Establish routines and make your room a place where students can count on knowing what to expect and what is expected of them. Having that degree of security will help them weather the storms of when truly unexpected things do happen.

IS HE JUST LAZY?

s your student lazy? Well, sometimes, but then, aren't we all? But before you label certain behaviors as simply lazy, let's look at what else might be going on.

Some autistic adults use the term "autistic inertia". It's like a form of procrastination. Think about when you procrastinate. When *I* procrastinate it could be for several reasons:

•It's a non-preferred task and I'd just rather be doing something else.

•"m not quite sure how to do it so am avoiding that state of insecurity when I have to stumble around, trying to figure it out.

•There's a deadline looming, and this just has to be done, but the task seems too enormous.

•It matters and if I mess it up, the consequences will not be good.

•I've had trouble with this in the past, didn't like that feeling so am trying to get out of doing it.

This is just a partial list; we all procrastinate at times. When you are autistic, all these same reasons may apply, on top of some other possibilities.

Has this student failed at something similar before? The

emotional barriers could be blocking him or her from trying again. Many autistic kids have faced social failure time and time again. How do you put yourself out there when it's hurt so much in the past?

~

Communication is a weak area for everyone on the autism spectrum, no matter how verbal they may seem. Even though you've given the direction over and over again, do they truly understand what is expected of them? Were they paying attention to your words or were they focusing on something else? Even though *you* assume that they know that this is a regular part of their routine, do they *actually* know this? This is the time to back up words with visuals - either pictures or written instructions. It's easier to take in and process visual information rather than oral.

Set up routines and yes, back up these routines with a visual schedule. The more things you can make routine the easier his day (and yours) will go.

Do not just assume that because you always do things this way or in this order that he has picked up on your routine. Use visuals. This includes not just creating the visual, but teaching what it is and referring to it often. Demonstrate how you go look at your schedule to see what you need to do next. Let him see you using your To Do list and how you use a schedule to organize your day.

~

This brings us to the subject of executive functioning. These are key skills that we need to manage our lives. Executive functioning includes our time sense, our ability to prioritize and to organize. It includes our ability to ignore distractors and to persist at a task. If you have great difficulty organizing yourself, tasks can seem monumental, making it easy to give up or not even try. You can help by breaking tasks into smaller pieces, writing those down and stroking a line through each as it is completed. (Again, don't just talk about it, but show it visually). Is there an essay or book report due? Chunk the component tasks along a timeline, with dates for when each part is to be tackled. Depending on the assignment, you might help him choose a topic by Monday, Tuesday write down all the subtopics that might be interesting about that topic. The next day, research and jot down notes about two of these topics, etc. If your child is technologically inclined, you might prefer to use an app or software program for this.

If you do an online search for mind mapping, you will find many options for a phone, tablet or computer. One example for young students is *Kidspiration*. If you're new to the concept of mind mapping here is an explanation. Here are 8 free mind mapping tools and ways to use them. *MindMup* is a free, online mind mapping tool. This article lists the best mind mapping tools of 2019.

~

Sensory issues interfere seriously with the lives of many autistic people. Most neurotypicals (those without a specific diagnosis) have good central coherence - the ability to weed out of the environment that which we don't need to pay attention to and to let the excess details fade away. But for those on the autism spectrum, often all the sensory inputs from the environment come at them with the same intensity. It takes a lot of concentration to consciously recognize, then choose to not attend to all those incoming, pesky messages. The hum of the air conditioning needs to be ignored even though it is just a prominent as the words you're saying to them. The dust particles from sun beams coming through the window partially obscure your face, making it difficult to look at you. The seam along the right toe of his sock is rubbing against his sneaker, irritating him and distracting his thoughts. As you can imagine, such a sensory load can make it hard to pay attention or even cause a person to freeze up. Or, understandably, to avoid certain situations or tasks.

〜

Throughout this book we talk about monotropism. Some of what we might see as non-compliance in our student might be more a sign of difficulty he is having tearing himself away from what his mind is thinking about. "Autistic inertia" might be part this and part a resistance to changing a state - difficulty starting, stopping or changing direction. While this can at times feel like a nuisance in the classroom, such intense focus can also lead to great things. Science teacher and autistic adult Fergus Murray[1] says, "Thinking in terms of inertia also gives some insight into the discomfort of being interrupted, or plans changing. It's as if we've loaded a cart to the brim with thoughts and feelings, and they we suddenly have to steer it round a sharp corner". He goes on to say, "Whatever interest is most aroused in a monotropic mind tends to pull in a whole load of processing resources. That naturally makes it harder to change track, especially when you understand that the paths of our thoughts always leave an imprint in our minds, and autistic ones leave deeper grooves than they might in the average mind."

〜

Overwhelmed and exhausted. Yes, that is often how autistic people feel. Remember that sleep issues are common for those on the autism spectrum and, chances are, your student arrives at school fatigued. On top of that just getting through the day can take all of their energy. You can see how they would need more down time than might someone else their age.

So, lazy? Perhaps sometimes. But more often what on the surface may look like laziness is really a reaction to weak executive functioning skills and all the influences that they are struggling with.

You can help by:

•creating routines,

•using visuals,

•breaking tasks into pieces,

•teaching organizational strategies,

•understanding his sensory issues and providing supports (see the chapter on sensory for more ideas),

•allowing for down time, and

•finding the relaxation strategies that work for him.

Listen[152] to this young woman's views on autism, depression and inertia.

There are more resources in the Reference section of this book.

WHAT IS STIMMING?

Stimming is short form for self-stimulation. It is a repetitive motion or activity an individual engages in with a fair degree of frequency.

It is not unusual for people to stim, especially when tense. Do you twirl a piece of hair? Tap your fingers? Jiggle your knee up-and-down? Continue stirring your coffee long after the sugar has dissolved? Do you smoke? Chew gum? These are all examples of repetitive behaviors. Sometimes we're conscious of doing them; at other times not. They can help us relax or self-regulate.

We might not particularly notice if someone is doing any of the above behaviors. It's when the repetitive behavior seems out of the norm that you might notice it.

One of the typical stims we associate with autism is hand flapping. Certainly, not every autistic person will flap their hands. And conversely, not everyone who flaps is autistic. Flapping is more common among young children, including neurotypical young children.

Another stim that we might associate with autism is rocking. Again, not not every individual who has an autism diagnosis will rock and, not everyone who finds rocking soothing is autistic.

Jumping, bouncing, twirling, moving fingers in front of the face or head banging are other common stims. Now, here's the thing about stims - for the most part, they are good for the student. If stimming keeps him calmer, you want that. If you're worried about the stim, consider these two questions:

- Is it harming the child?
- Is it harming anyone else?

If the answer to both questions is no, then leave well enough along.

You may have heard the phrase "quiet hands". Sometimes parents, teachers or therapists are bothered when a child flaps his hands. While there is nothing inherently harmful about hand flapping, these adults might worry that the behavior makes the child look different. It might embarrass the parents. There could be concern that by doing something to stand out from the crowd, he could become a target for teasing.

Hours and hours of therapy can go into trying to have the child cease with the hand motions. With all that you have to do, with all the challenging areas the child might experience in his life, is this the best way to spend his time? Is this the most pressing need in his life right now?

It is true that those hours of therapy might pay off and the child restricts his hand movements. The adults might *think* that this is an improvement, that he no longer looks so different. But what is the cost to achieve that bit of compliance? What are you telling that child? You've inferred that his natural way to express joy or to soothe himself is wrong or bad. Think about what receiving that message might do to your psyche. And, has he been given something to replace that behavior, something that suits him?

～

D yan[159] is a teacher and a mom to an autistic boy. Here's a video[1] she has made about stimming. Like Dyan, those of us who stand on the outside of autism peering in, can try to understand, wouldn't it be best to listen to what autistic adults tell us about stimming? And about suppressing those stims? Here's An Autistic Perspective on Stim Suppression[160].

Still not sure you quite get it about stimming? Think of it this way, and the functions it serves, in the words of science teacher and autist Fergus Murray:

"'Restricted, repetitive behaviors' are a natural response to feelings of instability. They allow you to assert control over what is happening and feel safer. This is probably a useful general rule, not something that's only true in autism – we see restricted, repetitive behaviors in all sorts of contexts, it's mostly just that autistic people's ones stand out as particularly odd, to most people." Fergus Murray[161].

Here are some articulate, autistic adults to help:

- What is Stimming? [162].
- Stimming? What's That? [163].
- Autistic Stimming[164].

A nd for more on how stimming helps your autistic student:

- What is Stimming and Why Do Autistic People Stim?[165].
- Sensory Overload and Why Stimming Helps[166].

WHY IS HE ALWAYS LATE?

I f you talk to him about this, you might want to think about your use of the word "always". Although he might be tardy frustratingly often, it is doubtful that he is late every single time he crosses your doorway. So, if you say "always" to him he might be confused or upset by that generalization because technically, it might not be true. Being autistic, he might take your words literally.

But that is an aside to the main topic. There could be several reasons behind his lateness. The first one might have to do with executive functioning. EF plays such a large role in the life of autistic students that it has a chapter of its own in this book.

Part of executive functioning has to do with a sense of time. If someone says to you "I'll meet you in ten minutes", even if you don't look at your watch, you have a pretty fair idea of when ten minutes will be up. If someone tells you that an essay is due in three weeks, your mind will automatically register roughly how much time you have to finish that project.

A person who has a weakness in executive functioning may have very little sense of the passage of time. They might not automatically feel the difference between five minutes, thirty minutes and sixty minutes. Some schools have a warning bell and then a few minutes later, a final bell. The first bell is to tell students to get to where they're supposed to be and if they're not there by the second bell they will be marked late. Most kids do not need to have this explained to them or, if it was explained, once when they were younger was sufficient for the message to stick. Don't assume this is true with your student who has autism, ADHD, learning disabilities, etc. Those subtle and unwritten rules might not have sunk in for them.

Sequencing goes along with this time perception. As part of our sense of time, we learn to sequence the days of the week, the months of the year, the periods in a school day, etc. Again, for most kids this comes naturally but for a child with weak EF these things are not so clear.

We have talked in other chapters about processing speed. Standing in front of a locker trying to decide which books you will need for the next period or two can be not a simple task for some kids. Think about all the steps involved in that seemingly simple act. Hopefully, that student has a schedule taped to the inside of his locker that he can refer to. That is way easier than having to memorize which day of the week it is and which subjects he has that day, as well as the order in which the periods come. But, let's say that the schedule is right there, and he knows what subject is coming up. The next task is to figure out what he needs to take along to that class. While that might be obvious to many students, it likely won't be to someone who has executive functioning challenges. A pen or some other writing implement should be a given. Then he will probably need a notebook and possibly the textbook for that class. The catch is that you have to realize that these items are required, and then you have to know where they are stored. You've seen the jumbled mess of some kids' lockers. Finding *anything* in there would be a daunting task.

Unfortunately, the tendency is often to grab a notebook. It might not be the correct notebook for that subject, but technically it is a book to write in. This is a disastrous move for any student who has organizational difficulties. He will end up with a mixture of math and history and science notes all in one book that he can't find when it comes time to study or review that subject. Some students find it easier if those subjects are color-coded. For example, if the math textbook is mainly white, a white notebook would match it for math. Science might have a red book etc. and note taped inside his locker could have a key reminding him which color goes with which subject.

As a teacher, have you ever thought about just how many pencils and pens you give out within a school year? Consider the size of a locker and think about the size of one pencil. Can you see how easy it would be to lose that pencil? Or, any of the half dozen his parents bought him at the start of the school year. One strategy is to keep a pencil case with needed implements inside the binder or notebook for each subject. Yes, that does mean purchasing more pencils pens and pencil cases but could save a lot of time and frustration. (Also, he would need to be taught the strategy of always returning those tools to their pencil case at the end of class).

So, his sense of time may be hindering him entering your classroom promptly and organizational difficulties at his locker could hamper him even more.

❧

S ensory issues could partly be the culprit here as well. Think about hallways in the school, especially at lunch, recess or break time. While you might have set routines and a quiet noise level maintained within your classroom, that is not always true in the hallways. There are many bodies moving in a small amount of space. For someone with visual sensitivities, all those colours and movement can be distracting. For a student who has auditory sensitivities the noise of the shuffling feet, the hushed or loud conversations, the laughing, the horsing around, not getting the social communication and innuendos, plus the anxiety of getting to the next class- well, it can all be overwhelming. Additionally, if your student has tactile sensitivities, he might be worried about someone either accidentally or intentionally brushing against him, which would send his nervous system into overdrive.

When his body is on high alert from such potential sensory threats, his ability to think and process other information will decrease. The sensory issues could overtake the cognitive parts of his mind leaving him little energy to remember what he was supposed to be doing in the hallway.

I know with some autistic kids who are consistently late. They are not intending to be disrespectful or disobedient, but they are protecting themselves. They might find a quiet place in the school to wait out the noise. Then, when the crowds have cleared out from the hallways, they will then go to their locker to get their materials. Yes, they are not strictly obeying the rules. But they are employing a strategy that will help keep somewhat calmer during your class rather than arriving at their desk in an over aroused state.

If your student is frequently late, talk to him about it. He might be oblivious to the fact that he's late. Perhaps he would be open to some strategies that you could suggest to better organize his locker and his belongings, strategies to get to help him get to where he supposed to be on time or strategies to avoid the chaos that might bother him in the hallways. It might be something as simple as letting him leave the classroom two or three minutes before the rest of the students so that he can gather his next books in the calmness of an empty hallway and make his way to the following class.

Maybe he is late because he is avoiding some students who are picking on him. Kids on the autism spectrum are frequently targets of bullies. Often, they are overly concrete thinkers and take things at face value. They can easily then become the butt of jokes. If they have tactile sensitivities, they might have freaked out in the past when people have touched them, and they couldn't take it anymore. Those kinds of weaknesses are magnets to bullies. Watch carefully, especially in the unstructured times at school to make sure that your student is not being victimized.

[167]For people with autism, time is a slippery concept.

WHAT IS EXECUTIVE FUNCTIONING?

⌒⧜⌒

We couldn't manage our lives without executive functioning skills. Executive functioning (EF) includes skills such as:

- managing time
- multi-tasking
- remembering things
- paying attention
- switching focus
- planning and organizing
- gathering and analyzing information to help guide our actions
- help governing our social responses

These can be broken into two broad areas of organization (including cognitive flexibility and regulation (inhibition). EF skills aren't just frills, or a nuisance when they're weak. They are critical to school life. The article, How Kids Use Executive Function Skills to Learn[168] illustrates this.

We need to be able to organize incoming and stored information in order to determine the best course of action to take. Say your doctor has suggested that you'd be better off and likely avoid the needs for medications if you lost twenty-five pounds. You've vegged out all day. Now the dog is nudging you to take him for a walk and you just spied an interesting movie on Netflix. Good executive functioning skills might help you to regulate your behavior, pointing it toward your end goal.

Our brain needs these EF skills in order to filter distractions, set and achieve goals, prioritize tasks, and curb impulsive behavior. For those of us who have decent EF skills, these are things we likely never think about. The abilities just come naturally. If you fall into that group, you are lucky but that makes it all that much harder to understand students who struggle with these issues. Here are 5 Common Myths About Executive Functioning Issues[169].

Students who have difficulties with EF might show problems in these areas:

- Planning projects
- Estimating how much time a project will take to complete
- Remembering directions, timelines, or where their belongings are
- Starting activities or tasks
- Shifting plans when situations change
- Keeping their attention only on what they need to be doing right then
- Shutting down when situations don't unfold as expected

. . .

An important one from the list above is starting activities. It's one we don't often think about. But there are students in your room who, although capable, have trouble completing their work on time. Perhaps EF is one of their stumbling blocks. Here's an interesting article on Why Kids with Executive Functioning Issues Have Trouble Starting Tasks. [170]

Another key area is memory, in particular working memory. You're using your working memory when you look up a phone number and hold it in your mind while you then dial that number. If you're unfamiliar with the term working memory, take a look at this article: Working Memory: What It Is and How It Works[171]. Those of you with keen working memories likely don't give this skill a second thought and don't consider how crucial it is in your classroom all day long. See 5 Ways Kids Use Working Memory to Learn[172].

In the chapter on auditory sensitivities, we talked about auditory processing difficulties. That is where a student might not find it easy to make sense of the words that he hears. Apart from the auditory realm, students can have difficult with processing speed in general. These are kids who, although they might get the concept, are slow to respond, slow to begin and complete work and struggle with the speed at which things move. If you wonder what this might feel like, take a look at A Day in the Life of a Slow Processing Child[173].

Imagine what a school day would be like for you if you always felt that you were behind everyone else, that they caught on faster and that things went by in a whirlwind. You might be frustrated and worried and anxious. Anxiety in general seems more prevalent in kids today but functioning with slow processing would make things worse. Slow Processing Speed and Anxiety: What You Need to Know[174].

Here are a couple short articles to sum up this section on processing speed:

- Slow Processing Speed Fact Sheet[175]
- Can Processing Speed Ever Improve? [176]
- How to Talk to Your Child About Slow Processing[177].

I f, like me, you like to know the neurology behind some of these things, here is an easy-to-read article on 4 Ways Brain Structure and Chemistry May Affect Processing Speed[178]. If you don't really care about the reasons why, just how you can help, check out this practical post on 7 Ways to Help Kids with Slow Processing Speed Take Notes in Class[179].

E F difficulties may present differently within different age groups. Here is some information on EF in various school levels:

- Executive Functioning Issues: What You're Seeing in your Grade-Schooler. [180]
- Executive Functioning Issues: What You're Seeing in your Middle-Schooler[181].
- Executive Functioning Issues: What You're Seeing in Your High-Schooler. [182]

Y ou might be getting a sense of just how weak EF might affect your student in the classroom as well as in the rest of his life. Sometimes we think that these are problems young children experience and they'll get better once they've been in school a few years. Possibly, for some kids, but often EF difficulties persist through life. Take a look at Everyday Challenges for Young People with Executive Function Challenges. [16] And, these effects don't end after high school. Read about How Executive Functioning Issues Affect Teens and Young Adults in the Workplace[183]. And, Everyday Challenges for Young Adults with Executive Functioning Issues[184].

〜

E xecutive functioning skills develop over time. Preschoolers have not yet developed this part of their brain efficiently. You may have noticed that youngsters of that age are impatient - they want what they want when they want it. Have you heard of the Marshmallow Test[19]? It's a famous experiment that has been replicated over and over, showing how some kids have developed the skill of delayed gratification while others have not. Take a look at the video clip here[185]. It will make you smile.

EF affects many aspects of a child's life, both in and out of school. Here is a summary of A Day in the Life of a Child with Executive Functioning Issues[186]. Executive functioning weaknesses can even impact a student's social skills. 4 Ways Executive Functioning Issues Can Affect Your Child's Social Life[187].

Self-regulation is a key skill we value in schools and need in life. Think about the EF skills of remembering information, cataloguing and comparing it then using that to govern your actions. Things can fall apart anywhere along this stage, making it harder for the person to regulate his emotional state. For EF and other reasons, this can be a tricky area for autistic people. This article is a nice read and will help you understand: Very Grand Emotions: How Autistics and Neurotypicals Experience Emotions Differently[188].

Think about the tasks involved in reading and how weak EF might interfere with reading[24] ability. The ability to plan is something that we take for granted and, we often admonish students to "plan ahead". But what if you don't exactly know what that means? Check out Why Kids with Executive Functioning Issues Have Trouble Planning[189].

E xecutive functioning skills include a sense of time. If someone tells you that they'll meet you in ten minutes, likely you have an internal sense of how long ten minutes is, even if you do not look at a watch. Having this sense of the passage of time can be a weak area for many autistic people. If an essay is due in two weeks, without that sense of time, the student could have little idea that a week and a half has gone by already. Teaching calendar skills can help. Talk about the calendar together how the days of the week are listed across the top and how each number represents a day. (Believe me; this is not obvious to all kids). Cross off each day before bed to help him get a sense of the passage of time.

W hile your student might come into your room with executive functioning issues, there are things you can do to help:

- First, be aware the directions like, "pay attention", "get down to work", "put your things away neatly", or even "listen" may be difficult for him.
- Remember to present information in a variety of ways. Don't rely on just oral directions, but couple them with examples and visuals.
- 10 Tips to Help Your Child Follow Directions[190].
- Not only does weak EF interfere with planning and task completion, but might lead to an atypical mindset. (Read

How Does the Child with Executive Function Issues
Think Differently[191]).

- Establish routines that the child can count on.
- Help him form effective habits.
- Don't assume that noncompliance is due to indifference.
- Is the Messy Backpack Due to Executive Functioning or
  Motivation Issues[192]?
- Executive Functioning Issues and Learning: 6 Ways to
  Help Your High Schooler. [193]

This age of technology can be a wonderful thing for those
with EF struggles. Most adults and many students own
smart phones or tablets. There are truly useful apps for these
things that can be a lifesaver when your EF is weak. Many do not
require any additional purchases and come already loaded on the
tablet or phone. Assistive Technology That's Built into Mobile
Devices[194].

I always like to listen to what articulate, adult autistic people
have to say on topics as they know this from the inside out and
generously share their knowledge and experiences with us. Here
are some to pay attention to:

- An Inside Look at Executive Functioning Issues[195].
- An Autistic Perspective on Autism and Executive
  Functioning[196].
- Ask an Autistic: What is Executive Functioning? [197]
- How Autistic People Can Achieve More in Their Life[198].

We'll end this chapter with resources for those of you who like delving into the brain science on these matters. Here are a few links to get you started:

- Developing Executive Function: What Happens in the Brain[199].
- Executive Functioning Issues and Possible Causes[200].
- Types of Tests for Executive Functioning Issues. [201]

And, if you want to learn more about EF without focusing on the neurology, here is a free book on Executive Functioning 101[202].

HOW CAN I HELP HIM BE LESS MESSY?

L et's first look at *why* your student might be "messy".
In school, we think of two broad categories of messy -
a child not keeping his belongings in an orderly fashion
and that student doing assignments that look messy.

W e'll first talk about why he may keep his desk and locker
messy. To organize those spaces requires decent
executive functioning skills, in areas such as memory, attention,
sequencing and spatial orientation. When he finishes his math
work sheet, it's time to put his pencil away and he might have that
job in mind. But the child sitting next to him asks him a question.
Now his attention is diverted to processing what his neighbor has
said and how to respond. Someone walks down his row, further
distracting him. Then the teacher directs the class to take out their
science books. That pencil gets dropped as he scrambles to comply
with the new directive. But, he didn't yet put his math sheet away,
so it gets hurriedly shoved inside his desk as he roots around,
trying to find his science book, pushing other materials aside in

the search. Now, his math work sheet has become trapped in that void and the pencil is who knows where.

To have handled this everyday occurrence better would have required good short-term memory. He would have needed to hold in his mind that he needed to put away his pencil. If he wasn't highly distractible and had good central coherence, then he could have conversed with his fellow student while putting his pencil in his case. If he had good sequential skills, he would have put his math sheet inside his math workbook and placed both neatly in their spot on the one side of his desk's interior. He would find retrieving his science book an easy task because all his notebooks were stacked tidily in one place.

Why would a child keep his desk like this? Is he lazy? Careless? Just doesn't care? Although it might *appear* that way, none of those things are likely the reason. Having a desk in that shape gets him in trouble. It's more work to find anything and the confusion adds to his frustration.

It's not only teachers who find this frustrating. Parents feel the same way about their child's backpack. They can't find notes from the school in it, their child's homework or that rotting orange. Even worse is when they slave away with their child on his dreaded homework, but it's finally completed and stowed in that backpack, never to be seen again. Take a look at this article: Is That Messy Backpack Due to Executive Functioning or Motivational Issues[206]?

Although he likely has weak executive functioning skills, life need not always be this disorganized for him. This is where systems and routines are so important. Drill over and over again where the students are always to place their items. Your autistic student will not be the only child in the room who has these same struggles. Here is a video[207] a first grade teacher made about training her kids to keep organized desks. Here are a few other ideas:

- Organizational Tips for Messy Student Desks [208]
- How to Organize Your School Desk[209]

F or more information on this, check out the chapter on executive functioning.

~

T hat student whose locker and desk are a mess might also turn in messy work. In this case, messy might refer to:

- paper that is crumpled
- paper that is torn
- paper that is dirty
- the corners of his notebook might be bent back
- the cover from his notebook might be partially ripped off
- his math questions might be on a paper that was meant for science notes
- his penmanship might be so poor that it's hard to make out his letters
- his letters don't follow the lines on the page
- his sentences slope up to the left or right
- the page is torn because he has erased so much that the paper is worn through
- his writing does not begin at the left-hand margin
- he makes arithmetic errors because his numbers are not lined up in rows

. . .

Gross and fine motor coordination are often weak areas for autistic students. A good part of this is due to differences in their cerebellum, which we'll discuss in a minute.

But you want to know what you can do to improve his hand writing. Here are a few suggestions:

- Make sure that he is sitting at a desk that is correctly sized for him. His legs should not be dangling. His feet should fit firmly on the floor. If his legs are too short, place a stool, box or even books under his shoes so that his feet are flat on the floor.
- Many autistic kids have low muscle tone in general and weak trunk muscles. This makes it hard for them to sit and maintain themselves upright in a chair for extended periods of time. Allow him to get up, walk around and change his posture so that he's not overly fatigued from trying to constantly sit up straight.
- Elevate the front of his desk so that his book sits at a slant. Propping his paper on a four-inch binder might work. You can purchase ready-made slant boards or make your own. If you are unfamiliar with slant boards, here are a couple to look at:

Https://amzn.to/2KFrWGU.
https://amzn.to/2Z270z6.

- Have him write on the board. Sometimes a vertical surface is less tiring than writing on a horizontal desk.
- Younger kids might like laying on their stomach on the floor to do their written work.

- The width of their writing utensil could make a difference. Experiment with different sizes of pencils, markers and pens.
- Pencil grips can also make a big difference to the quality of a child's handwriting. Here is a two-minute tutorial from an occupational therapist on pencil grips for kids. [210] Pencil grips come in a dizzying array of sizes and shapes, and with good reason. You'll need to experiment to see which are helpful for your student. Here[6] are a few examples. Please keep in mind your student's age. What will fit in just fine in a grade one classroom will not be cool in grade ten.
- Does he need to use a pen and paper to complete his work? Could he use a computer? A netbook? A tablet?
- Could he dictate his work? Some ways to do this are described in the chapter, But I Teach High School.

Here[210] is an article that will explain more about why your student might have messy handwriting.

Apart from his handwriting, why would his written work be such a mess? It might have something to do with his cerebellum. The cerebellum is a lobe in your brain, near the back, above your neck. It is important for coordination and motor learning. When a child first learned how to print, his efforts are slow and laborious. Over time, with practice, his neurons learn the mechanics of forming those letters and they require less and less conscious thought, until the skill becomes automatic. This is the same type of learning we go through when we learn how to play a musical instrument or a dance step.

But, with autistic kids, there are cerebellar differences at both the neuronal and structural level. (If you find neurology fascinating, take a look at this article[214]).

While the cerebellum plays an important role in coordination and motor learning, it is also involved in other things such as memory and socialization[9]. To delve into this a bit more, check out this article on the role of the cerebellum in autism[215].

A lthough the cerebellum takes up only about ten percent of our brain, eighty percent of the brain's neutrons are involved there. Here is a nice video clip about The Cerebellum, Autism and How the Human Brain Gets Organized[216].

The cerebellum in autistic kids differs from that of their peers. Before you let anyone suggest that your student is lazy or doesn't care, remind them of this basic brain structure and how it likely affects your student. The cerebellum's affects go far behind just fine and gross motor coordination.

It was once thought that this irregularly shaped structure of the brain primarily governed motor function, but recent studies suggest that it also plays an important role in implicit learning (extracting the underlying rules without explicit instruction) as well as sensory and cognitive function [217].

WHAT IF HE WON'T EAT AT SCHOOL?

Y ou might also have an autistic student who is hungry, but not because he has not been offered food at home. There are many sensory issues involved in eating, from taste, the texture of the food, its temperature, smells, and even colors. Worries about their child's eating habits occupies much of some parents' time.

Some kids might prefer to only eat soft foods. Others might find anything mushy abhorrent in their mouths. You will find more information about this in the chapter that has to do with the gustatory sensitivities.

Apart from the taste and feel of foods in the mouth, there are auditory factors that can make eating difficult for some autistic kids. As mentioned in the auditory chapter, some kids with autism have acute hearing. The smallest sound that might not even register on our consciousness is readily discernible to them. An example is the chewing sounds that others make. If that sound is really bothersome, it might put the child off eating. Smells can also be a problem with eating at school. When students open their lunch bags, all sorts of aromas can mingle in the air. If you have a very keen olfactory sense, then some of these smells could be off-putting.

L unchtime is often a noisy time of day, where many kids relax and socialize with their friends. That level of noise, the expectation of social interaction, not quite getting the social stuff, and the layers of so many conversations going on at once can all be overwhelming for a child with autism. Some handle it by almost going inside themselves, trying to tune out the confusion that is happening around them and their own eating falls by the wayside.

Keep in mind that executive functioning skills are weak areas for most autistic kids. Part of executive functioning is activation - the ability to begin a task. Class is over for the morning and lunch time begins. The students all pull out their lunches and begin to eat, except for that child who has difficulty with activation. He might spend five minutes just looking around or fidgeting with something. Then he will realize, or someone will remind him, that he should go get his lunch. He walks to his locker and stands there looking in, lost in thought and reflecting on some of the papers he has in there, his favorite jacket that his grandma bought him and then he reaches for his lunch bag. There are also some distractions between the locker and his desk so it might take him another five minutes before he is back sitting down and ready to eat. Unzipping his bag, he looks at the array of possibilities. Some might appeal to him; some might be things that his mom has said he must eat. Maybe he hast to brace himself, knowing that there are some items in there that will be hard for him to get down.

Finally, he begins and then the bell rings. The teacher says it's time to put your lunch away and go out to play at recess. Trying to be obedient, he zips his lunch bag back up and puts it away and slowly trails the others out of the room.

. . .

N ow, as a teacher you cannot force a child to eat. No one can make a kid eat. And, you should not try. But you know the effect that being hungry will have on this child's learning and possibly behavior, that afternoon.

What you can do for him is be aware of the factors that might make eating lunch difficult for him. Talk to his parents and find out what works at home. Talk to the child; tell him that you noticed he wasn't eating much. Ask if he can tell you why. Ask him what would make eating lunch easier for him.

D epending on what is comfortable for that child and his family, he might prefer to eat lunch in a different location - one that is quieter, with fewer people and distractions. Maybe he needs a private signal between the two of you that will remind him when it is time to go get his lunch. Maybe eating a meal simply takes longer for him and he might be given extra time, missing some of the recess.

Maybe the student would do better eating smaller meals spread out across his school day. Perhaps part of his lunch would be eaten mid-morning, some at lunch, and some mid-afternoon. Maybe his parents would agree to keeping a supply of food for him at the school for those days that he does not want to eat what is in his lunch.

Due to interoception weaknesses, your student may not be able to read the signs that tell him he is hungry. Just as with toilet training difficulties, this child might learn to eat on a schedule, rather than relying on his body's signals. Meal time can be written into his visual schedule. (This could also apply to drinking water).

WHY DOES HE REMIND ME OF A STUDENT WITH ADHD?

I f you are noticing similarities, you are likely right. Some autistic kids also have a diagnosis of attention deficit hyperactivity disorder. Some do not have a separate diagnosis but definitely share some commonalities with kids who do.

Kids with ADHD do not actually have a *deficit* of attention; rather they pay too much attention. Everything snags their attention, interfering with those things we want them to attend to.

We've talked in other chapters about weak central coherence and how autistic kids can find it difficult to block out the tiny details and focus on the "big picture". This can be similar to how ADHD kids have trouble weeding out distractions and attending to the task we have set for them.

We often think of ADHD kids as having short attention spans. Again, this is because as they begin to focus, other things interfere, taking their attention off-task. This can also be true of autistic kids.

Conversely, we often see kids who have an ADHD diagnosis who are able to focus extraordinarily well on certain things that they find intensely interesting. This is also true of autistic students, especially when operating within their areas of interest. Their attention is fully taken up with that activity and they can be oblivious to what else is going on. Here's an article on attention and monotropism[218]. Listen to what Damian Milton[219] has to say about this as he talks about monotropism[3] and these flow states.

Much of what we think of as "paying attention" is part of our set of executive functioning skills. These involve our sense of time, our ability to plan and sequence. When skills like these are weak, you can see how a student might come across as inattentive, scattered and disorganized. We go into this in more detail in the chapter on executive functioning.

WHY IS HIS HYGIENE POOR?

❦

This is less of a problem in the younger grades, but as adolescence hits, attention to hygiene becomes much more important. Gently suggesting to the parents that work on their child's hygiene may result in this question: "How do I get him to shower?" (Yes, I know that questions such as these are *not* the reason you went into teaching. Nonetheless, you may still be asked).

The first answer that comes to my mind is, "With great difficulty." But, I suspect you already know that. This is a common concern with adolescents and teens and not just with boys. Here are some things that you might discuss with the parents.

There are several things at play here. The first is sensory and the second is interoceptive. Interoception is not as well known; it is the ability to read your body's internal states and often in autism, it is slow to develop. This includes reading the signs that you are hungry, thirsty, tired, in pain, etc. When we're in need of a shower, most of us begin to feel uncomfortable. Even if we don't stink, our scalp becomes itchy as oils build up and we know that our skin will feel better after showering. But, if you are unable to register and decode these body signals, you won't realize that you are feeling badly and you'll feel better after bathing. And, even though his body odor might offend others, odds are that that child does not smell it himself.

Another related issue is changing clothing. There's not much point bathing if you then put on the same shirt you've been wearing and sweating in for days. The rule is you change your underwear and socks daily - even if they look clean and are your most comfortable ones. Rules are rules and must be followed even when you don't like them or understand the reason why they're there. (That is a handy parenting and teaching trick to learn - "The rule is...".)

The bathroom is a nasty place for anyone with sensory sensitivities. Because of all the porcelain and tile, it tends to be a noisy, echoing space. Sound bounces off the walls. For those with visual sensitivities, light also reflects. The bathroom is full of smells - cleanser, shampoo, soaps, lotions, etc. This room might already have negative connotations if brushing teeth was an issue earlier on (due to oral/motor sensitivities). Then there is the tactile sensation of water pounding down on your skin.

Most people on the autism spectrum are rule-followers. Once the rule is ingrained, they tend to follow it. So, the rule is that you shower each morning. Or evening or alternate days or whatever is appropriate in their house. Mark it on a calendar and his daily/weekly schedule. It simply must be done before he gets to do the things that he enjoys.

Saying, "Go shower" might not be enough. I know of kids who come out of the bathroom with wet hair but when it dries, it's still greasy. While they might have stood in the shower that does not mean that they washed themselves. Likely, they require more guidance. You could make a step-by-step list such as:

• Put shower curtain in the tub (or whatever to keep the water from going on the floor)

• Turn on shower taps and adjust water to right temperature (remember with interoception problems he could easily make it too hot or too cold without realizing it)

• Take off your clothes and get in under the water spray so that you are all wet

• Pour a bit (you might need to be exact about how big a dab is) of shampoo on your hand then rub it all over your head (standing erect while tolerating the water plus keeping his eyes shut might tax his vestibular system so you might consider baby shampoo that won't sting his eyes)

• Rinse out the shampoo (adding conditioner to the mix might be a bit much)

• Take the soap and rub it in your underarms and groin area

• Rinse the soap off

• Turn off the water and get out of the tub

• Use your towel to dry off

• Comb your hair

Put on clean clothes.

These are just examples of what you might suggest to the parents for a list. Laminate the page or place it in a Ziploc bag and hang it from the shower head or on the wall. Show it to him and go over and over it. Be firm about the time frame about when he must shower but allow him some choice (such as before bed or upon arising in the morning).

The tricky thing is also that sensitivities don't remain constant - they can lessen or grow stronger, depending on the stressors in the person's life and the maturity of their nervous system. Here are a few things to try. Smells were a huge issue for a teen. His mom would take him to a drug store, and they'd stand there opening and smelling deodorants. Sometimes one smell would overwhelm him so much that he could not take any more and they'd need to go home and try again a different day. They finally narrowed it down to one brand that didn't bother him quite as much. Thought the problem was solved until he started avoiding even that kind. Back to the store. They discovered a deodorant stone. It came in a plastic case and is a whitish soft stone; you wet it and rub it on your underarm. It has no odor. It may not be as effective as most commercial deodorants, but it seemed to work. Drug stores and health food stores carry it.

Just like with the deodorant, they may need to spend quite some time finding a soap and shampoo whose scent does not disagree with their child. Sometimes health food stores carry unscented types. Baby shampoo might have fewer chemical smells. Or, you might run across an aroma that appeals to him, such as fruity body soap. Some body washes can even double as shampoo.

~

If you search online, you can find social stories about showering. These are just a few:
- Autism and Hygiene: Sensory Overload. [221]
- Personal Hygiene[222].
- Personal Hygiene Social Story[223].
- How to Take a Shower[224].

[221] Autism and Hygiene: Sensory Overload http://youtu.be/sJIiZhDdkO4.
[222] Personal Hygiene www.adders.org/socialstories5.htm.
[223] Personal Hygiene Social Story www.youtube.com/watch?v=fsT3sEjtdME.
[224] How to Take a Shower www.youtube.com/watch?v=dcCVfaLkzJk.

HOW DO I EXPLAIN TO HIS CLASSMATES?

erhaps you don't. If kids have come up through the grades together, they already know that he is different.

Autism is a medical diagnosis and as such that information is confidential. Until that child reaches the age of majority, the parents are the determiners of who they might or might not choose to share that information with. There are parents who do not want the school staff to know. Other parents will allow the current teacher to be aware of the diagnosis. Others are fine with the adults in the building being aware.

But, you do not have permission to tell that diagnostic information to that child's classmates.

Sometimes a parent will want you to share their child's diagnosis with his peers. Carefully discuss this with them. One of the parents might wish to come present to the class (perhaps with their child not being present). Others will be uncomfortable talking in front of a group of kids and ask that you or your designate do it. If this is the parent's wish, I would suggest discussing it with your autistic student first to make sure that he is in agreement.

· · ·

There might be no need to talk about autism in your room. If you set up a climate where differences are made ordinary, all students will be accepted. They'll understand that they all have individual strengths and challenges and that they all learn in slightly different ways and that that is all right. They'll respect that each student is a valued, contributing member of the group even when their participation might vary. An atmosphere like this takes the pressure off many of the kids in your room.

~

This might be a time to bring up empathy. There is a myth that autistic don't have empathy.

Just as your autistic student might have trouble reading the mind of someone else, you might have equal difficulty knowing what is in his mind. How Easy Is It to Read the Minds of People with Autism Spectrum Disorder? [225]

In fact, their empathy might look different but can be deep. Read about the Double Empathy Problem by Dr. Damian Milton[226].

Part of the confusion around autism and empathy might have to do with alexithymia[227] and Theory of Mind. Here is a video[228] that does a good job of explaining this, from an autistic perspective. And here is Dr. Todd Grande's explanation of alexithymia[229].

WHAT WILL HAPPEN TO HIM
WHEN HE FINISHES SCHOOL?

W ill he be able to live on his own? Good question. That depends on him (or her), the views and goals of the parents and the transition planning that has occurred long before he leaves the school system.

You see, there is a <u>wide spectrum of abilities</u> among autistic people. Roughly half of those diagnosed with autism have cognitive ability (or IQs) in the average to above average range. And, about half have some degree of intellectual disability ranging from mild to profound. Many people with mild intellectual disabilities and perhaps some with moderate ID are able to live independently with varying degrees of assistance.

There are definitely those who have both autism and an intellectual disability but determining that is not clear cut. You see, we determine level of intellectual functioning by using intelligence tests. The most common one you might hear of is the WISC (Wechsler Intelligence Scale for Children) or the WAIS (Wechsler Adult Intelligence Scale). They look at various ways we think and reason, including our working memory, processing speed, verbal comprehension and perceptual reasoning.

As you are aware, some people on the autism spectrum are nonverbal and cannot use speech for communication. Others are more able to express themselves using words sometimes, but when anxious or becoming overwhelmed, the use of speech is more difficult for them.

The problem with intelligence tests and autism is that some of the test parts require verbal skills, meaning that the individual has to answer orally. There are some ways around this and a nonverbal (not requiring spoken responses) form can be given. This somewhat takes care of the verbal requirement, but there is still another problem.

Even if the speech requirement is removed, or with those who do communicate orally, when taking an IQ test, the individual must be able to understand what the examiner says and what is required of them. While hearing might not be a problem, auditory processing often is. Although the person can hear just fine, making sense of the words he hears may not always be easy. Auditory processing is more difficult under noisy, disruptive conditions but intellectual assessments are usually conducted in a quiet atmosphere.

The ability to process is also affected by anxiety and the testing situation itself is anxiety-producing. Often the test is conducted by a stranger in an unfamiliar room. The process itself is intimidating.

If those factors are all fine for the person being tested, there is pacing. Many autistics trying to make sense of things, find that the world moves at a fast pace - too fast for their comfort. By the time they have worked out what is going on and what may be expected of them, others have moved on to the next thing. Parts of the IQ tests are timed with bonus points for finishing more quickly and lower points being awarded (or penalized) for those who take beyond the expected seconds or minutes to complete the task.

An autistic mind might not travel along the same path as that of the neurotypical examiner. While there are certain sets of questions and items to go through, in a certain order, the autistic person being examined might not follow along. Something the examiner says or asks, or part of the test might take the testee's mind down a different avenue, something of interest to that person - something far more interesting than the task the tester has set out. Time may be lost as the person focuses on something that caught his fancy and he may miss instructions, complete a task in the wrong way or lose out on timed points.

Many people on the autism spectrum have difficulty with executive functioning. EF skills involve such things as our sense of time, our ability to maintain our focus and to shift attention appropriately. EF involves other things, but these ones particularly affect performance on an intellectual assessment.

Fatigue also sets in. Undergoing such testing is not fun and is fatiguing for anyone. But if you are autistic and must put in extra effort to control your attention and play along with someone else's agenda for hours, it will become hard to maintain focus. None of us perform at our best when tired and/or anxious.

This is a very long way of saying that while intelligence tests are the best measures we have right now to assess a level of intellectual functioning, they have flaws and are not necessarily accurate with the autistic population.

∾

Are you wondering when we will get to whether or not your student will be able to live on his own? We're getting there. It depends partly on his level of intellectual functioning. Someone with a profound intellectual disability will require a much higher degree of care all his life than someone whose ability is closer to the average range.

But IQ alone will not determine if an individual can live independently. As we discussed above, the scores from an IQ test may not tell the full story of how a person functions.

There are autistic people who, when young, presented as if they had an intellectual disability, but later in life this was clearly not true. Dr. Temple Grandin is an example. Sometimes individuals who are nonverbal and unable to use spoken language to communicate their wants and needs might come across as lower functioning. A few other examples are Stephen Shore, [1] Carly Fleischmann[2] and Amanda Baggs[3].

My advice is to never assume. Never assume that your student is incapable or does not understand. I find it sad when adults talk about a child in his presence as if he cannot hear nor understand what they are saying. Too often, teachers talk to each other in the hallway about kids, or in front of a nonverbal student. It's rude. Even if the child does not understand the words, he might pick up on your tone or attitude. But what if he *does* understand but just can't communicate that to you? There are instances of adults who are now articulate in some form (verbally or in writing) who can recall what was said about them in front of them when they were children.

I am not implying that hiding inside every autistic person is a budding genius. This is not true of the general population and neither is it true among those with autism. But the way your student seems to you at age four when you compare him to other preschoolers is not necessarily the way he will be compared to his peers at age fourteen or twenty-four or thirty-four. Don't assume. And by that, I mean don't assume *anything*.

≈

Now, let's skip ahead a decade or two. Your student's time in the school system is coming to a close. During parent-teacher interviews, his parents ask if you think he will live under their roof forever. That's a tough question.

It is unlikely that he will finish his stint in high school and then move out on his own to begin his adult life at age eighteen. Or, if he does, it might not be successful. (Again, there are no rules. This will depend on how prepared he is). Many typical young adults find the move to adult life difficult, but this is even more true of those on the autism spectrum.

An abrupt transition from living under his parents' care to taking up the reins of adult life independently is a huge step that many young people struggle with. The difficulty and stress would be multiplied vastly if your adult child has autism.

Instead, work towards this transition must begin early, way early. Adolescence may even be late to begin looking toward adult life.

Think of the skills needed to live life on a day-to-day basis then begin teaching those. At home, when young, the child should have the opportunity to make choices, starting with the clothes he puts on, etc., being held accountable for his choices, helping him to see the pros and cons of the options.

Although this might not seem strictly part of school academics, parents will often ask their child's teacher about such things and share their worries for the future. Encourage these parents to give their child responsibilities; everyone in the home can contribute to the functioning of the house in some way. Responsibilities increase as the child ages. Both at home and at school, do not do for the child something he can do for himself. Yes, it takes longer, and the result might not look as pretty but learning independence is crucial.

When their child is different, it is natural for a parent to over-protect. If their child is often passive, they can slide into the habit of doing too much for him. I know a little boy who had been in school for two years. At first, his mom brought him to his classroom daily and met him at his desk after school. She would tidy up and put away his belongings and help him into his jacket. Gradually, the teacher encouraged the mom to wait outside the classroom door, then later, outside the school door. She'd have the mom peak around the door to watch her son following his visual schedule that directed him in where to store his books, pencils and crayons, then the steps involved in putting on his jacket and book bag. In the mornings, a cheery staff member would meet the mom and boy as they came into the school, playfully waving the mom off, assuring her that they'd take care of her son. Initially, the lad would hold up his foot for the staff person to remove his shoe, just as he'd do for his mom. He'd stand placidly waiting with his arms at his sides for someone to take off his coat for him. Within a short period of time, he was pulling off his own shoes and placing them on the boot rack. He'd remove his jacket and place it on the hook in his cubby. (But when his mom was around, he'd revert to waiting for her to do these things for him).

When the teacher discussed independence skills and the importance of working now toward future transitions, the mom explained that she liked doing things for him. She felt that life was so hard for her child that she needed to help him as much as she could. It took another year before this student became impatient waiting for his mom and he'd tell her, "I can do it myself." His mom's feelings were hurt; she felt that he was rejecting her. The teacher and school guidance counsellor worked with the mom on other ways she could build on that feeling of togetherness with her child and the need to help him.

Once at a conference I chatted with a mom whose son would be attending college in a few months. She was so enthused and proud of her son's ability. His college had a residential program for autistic and learning disabled students; we were here to listen to their presentation. The college reps talked about the accommodations and assistance they'd extend to students in their program. At the end of the talk this mom raised a hand and asked a question, "But who will do his laundry?" There was silence. Oh dear. I appreciate that she was so proud of her son's intelligence and high-grade point average. But what is the point of being smart if you don't have the life skills to be able to do anything with those smarts?

Laundry is one of those pesky management things we all need to do. It's a skill that can easily be taught, especially when enhanced by visuals. Even young children can help transfer clothes from the washing machine to the dryer.

I met the parents of a young autistic woman who was thirty. She had successfully completed high school, a bachelor's degree at university and then a Master's degree in music. But her self-management skills were woefully lacking. Lucky for her, her parents were well off financially. They described to me what they had in place. They bought her a three-bedroom condo. One bedroom was for their daughter, the second was her music room and the third, along with its ensuite was for the paid companion who resided there to take care of their daughter.

They had a variety of other part-time employers to assist this young woman. One did all her grocery shopping, clothing and personal shopping and her laundry. A housekeeper came in daily to clean and to cook. Another woman arrived early each morning to get their daughter out of bed, coax her through dressing, hygiene and breakfast then took the bus with her to her part-time job. Once there, a job coach took over, spending four hours with her as she performed clerical work in an office. Then, the morning woman returned at noon to accompany the daughter on the bus back home. A trust fund was set up to continue this assistance permanently.

Not many of us are in financial positions to be able to spend this degree on money. Was it necessary? Her parents definitely believed so. They did not think she was capable of acquiring any of these skills on her own despite having been able to complete an advanced degree at university. I wonder....

Most kids will need to acquire some degree of independent and self-management skills. Even those who will reside in a group home will be expected to contribute to the running of the house.

A few examples of skills that can be taught are:
- how to organize and clean your bedroom
- how to wash dishes
- how to cook
- how to shop for groceries
- how to budget money
- how to clean a house
- how to open and manage a bank account and/or credit card

~

When their child is different, there is a tendency to over-protect. They know that life is harder for him and want to do what they can to help. Sometimes that urge to protect takes the form of doing things for him. While kind, providing "good care" might not be what he needs. Opportunities to learn how to care for himself might be more valuable.

What is the point of being smart if you can't manage your life enough so that you can make use of those smarts?

Schools are concerned with preparing students for life, in whatever form that life might take. Most individual education plans have a transition component built in. While individual academic achievements might be important, none of our curricular goals are more important than that student being able to manage his life to the best of his ability. Partnering with parents and planning transitions is vital.

You don't want this to be true of your student: "We have seen many individuals whose natural talents are wasted due to their untreated social disability and other weaknesses (e.g. inability to manage the practical aspects of independent living." [4]

. . .

S tephen Shore https://www.youtube.com/watch?v= 0teFbz4TB-A.

Carly Fleischmann https://www.chatelaine.com/living/real-life-stories/my-daughters-severe-autism-and-how-she-found-her-voice/.

Amanda Baggs https://well.blogs.nytimes.com/2008/02/28/the-language-of-autism/.

WILL HE EVER HOLD DOWN A JOB?

You're a teacher and teachers ultimately prepare students for their life after school. You might wonder if this applies to your autistic student. Will he be able to hold down a job? That is another good question and, like many of the others, it depends. Much of it depends on the individual's level of functioning as well as the skills he has acquired.

Level of functioning applies to a number of different things. In psychological terms, level of functioning often refers to cognitive ability or IQ level. (We covered some of this in the chapter Is He High Or Low Functioning?) If you read that, then you might want to skip to the next section of this chapter to see how it applies to the world of work).

IQ stands for intellectual quotient. This is usually derived from a standardized IQ test. Some of the most common IQ tests are the Wechsler Adult Intelligence Scale (WAIS) for people age sixteen and up and for kids the Wechsler Intelligence Scale for Children (WISC) is used.

While very few people will say that these are exact and accurate measures of a person's intelligence, for now they're the best tool that we have. But for people on the autism spectrum the results are even more suspicious. It's not uncommon to meet autistic people who have scored quite low on one of the Wechsler IQ tests yet when people work with them; they see skills that would not be expected for someone functioning at that low of a level.

Some of the difficulties with IQ tests and people with autism are related to their language ability. Some autistic people are nonverbal, meaning that they don't use spoken words to communicate. They might communicate quite well through some sort of assistive technology or typing or gestures or a picture system but not by talking. About half of the subtests involved in a Wechsler IQ test require spoken responses. Now, some clinicians do administer a Wechsler allowing non-spoken responses. For example, the person might type out what they want to say. This is breaking the standardization of the test so the results are somewhat suspect, but at least it gives you an indication of how that person might be thinking and how they respond to the test items.

Even with those individuals who do speak there might be other language problems. You need the ability to understand what is said to you in order to follow the oral directions on the Wechsler tests. Some people are able to grasp of the requirements by watching the demonstrations with the physical materials but understanding what is said orally would make that much easier.

Timing is another aspect. Some of the items on the Wechsler are timed responses meaning that the individual must respond within a certain amount of time in order to get points for that question. And there are bonus points for responding promptly and accurately.

Many autistic people have difficulties with executive functioning and with processing speed so they may understand the task but comply slowly, it may take them a while to figure out what is required, but in the end they can do it accurately. Still others will have difficulty understanding what the examiner says.

Also, along with executive functioning is the ability to manage attention. This can be problematic for some autistic people. For one, it requires joint attention which is the examiner and the examinee both focusing their attention on the same thing at the same time. Some people being tested are more observant of their own internal thoughts which may not run along the line of what the test is requiring hence slowing down their response or having them not respond at all. For example, if the person has an inner dialogue or monologue running and the examiner asks a question that requires a spoken response, the person might give a response that is based on the thoughts in his own mind rather than the response the examiner requests.

The point of this lengthy discussion is related to IQ some people with an autism diagnosis also legitimately have an intellectual disability that might range from profound to mild. Most people with a severe or profound intellectual disability are not engaged in paid work. That does not mean that they don't necessarily contribute in any fashion. Some people residing in group homes who require a considerable amount of daily care also contribute in those group homes by doing chores such as setting the table, emptying the dishwasher, etc.

It is generally assumed that the higher the IQ, the higher the potential the individual has for learning and later on for working. Now, it certainly is not a black-and-white line here and there are many, many variables

Back to the terms low functioning and high functioning. (We spent some time on this in a previous chapter but will go over it briefly in case you skipped that chapter).

There is quite a controversy within the autism community about this. There are those individuals who are supposedly deemed low functioning who in fact process at a much higher level than people would expect. Examples of this are Amanda Baggs and Carly Fleischmann. (You can view one of Amanda's videos here[1]: and one of Carly's videos here[2]).

Even those people on the autism spectrum who are deemed

"high functioning" often readily admit that they are not high functioning in all aspects every day. It can change and change quickly and unpredictably. Most often this has to do with anxiety and/or sensory sensitivities. Someone may manage to hold together under ordinary circumstances but then something comes along that impacts their sensory sensitivities hugely so that they feel overwhelmed. Then, while in that state, they are no longer able to function at a high level meaning their normal coping mechanisms and skills for managing themselves keeping their emotions and reactions regulated and just functioning in their day-to-day life are greatly diminished.

But it is in just such an environment that some autistic adults are finding success. Chef Tom Dickinson[3] is an example. So, as always with autism, never assume. Let the person be guided by his interests and skills.

～

Despite potentially having the skills, ability and education to be successful at some jobs, the employment rate for autistic people is frighteningly low. Here[4] is a good article on why the autistic *un*employment rate is so high.

There are some jobs that carry with them the requirement of socialization. This could be trying for many on the autism spectrum. While someone with autism might be friendly and have the need for a certain number of friendly encounters, nonstop rubbing shoulders with other people can be challenging. (And not just for those who have autism).

Processing speed enters into this as well. If you are going to be a receptionist in a busy office, you must be able to multitask well and do it all rapidly. You might be required to man the phones, operating several different lines at the same time, keeping track of whom you have put on hold, which caller you are transferring to and take down any required messages. That can be a stress-producing situation for many people. On the other hand, if someone can manage the pace and multitasking, in that job the individual's social contacts with others might be limited in both time and the quality of interactions. The interactions might require courtesy and speed and a short number of sentences but that's all, which could suit some employees.

This new world of online commerce and contract work is a real boon for many on the autism spectrum. They can work from home, maybe even in their pajamas, and often at whatever hours suit them. The drawback to such contract work is that rarely does it come with the benefits such as health care pension etc. And it requires a certain degree of multitasking because while you're working on one contract you need to be always chasing the next one so that you will have some work lined up for when you have completed the first job. If someone has the executive functioning skills to manage, this working from home can be ideal.

Many people who have an autism diagnosis and post-secondary education are under-employed. This means that they are likely not doing a job that requires the skills and knowledge that they obtained during their post- secondary training. There are a couple of reasons for this.

It's one thing to be able to do well in an academic setting, acquiring and demonstrating those skills. It's another thing to be able to carry those skills into the work environment. Some find the work part of it just too stressful and choose to then take a job that requires not as much thinking power, concentration, socialization, organization, etc.

There's another reason why some of these bright, competent autistic adults are not working in their trained fields. The thing is, first they have to land the job. And in most situations, you land that job initially through an interview.

The interview process is not an easy one for most autistic individuals. Interviews require a lot of reading between the lines trying to determine what exactly the interviewer is getting at and what would he like you to say. Often interview questions are open-ended leaving the interviewee unsure of what is wanted or the direction in which the questions are heading. So, the job candidate might give what he believes is a full answer but in doing so talk on and on and on, boring the interviewer or not allowing the company person to get another question in. "Full disclosure" to an autistic person might mean exactly that and he will confess to every error he has ever made. In his effort to be as accommodating and forthright as he could, he might have lost himself the job. Having a portfolio of work to take a long can be really helpful because then the company can see examples of exactly what the person is capable of.

There are a few other difficulties autistic people will face when getting a job. Let me give you an example. A dad once said to me about his young adult son, "he won't do anything he doesn't want to. He won't do anything he doesn't see the point of." Then he went on to explain that "see the point of" means something that's meaningful and interesting to his son.

Any of you who hold a job know that no matter how much you might enjoy the work and enjoy the challenges there will be parts of that job that you do not enjoy. That's just part of life; there are things that we all have to do that we do not feel like doing but must get done anyway. It's the rare person who gets to do only what they want to do.

Well I certainly understand this dad's point of view and the fact that his son only wants to do those things that interest him, sadly, life just does not work that way. So, this young man is not able to hold down a job, even a part-time job. He wants to just pick the parts of a task that appeal to him at that particular moment; what appeals varies day-to-day. That's likely true of most of us, that then there is the "suck it up factor". We just have to do certain things whether or not we like them or whether or not we feel like it at the present time; they still need to get done, because that's just part of the whole parcel.

I hear this in schools as well when we're talking about autistic students. I've been a teacher and I know many teachers. Most try very hard to make their students' lives and their assignments as interesting as possible but sadly, it is not possible to appeal to everyone all of the time. And there are just things that need to get done. In school there are ways to adapt, accommodate and offer alternatives for sure; still, there are times when you are expected to do something whether or not it appeals to you. That's also a fact in the working world.

Not being able to do things whether or not you feel like it can be a real hindrance to finding and keeping a job. You may have heard of PDA. PDA stands for Pathological Demand Avoidance[5]. While this is not a diagnostic label in any of our medical books, it is a term used by some parents and other professionals working with kids who have autism. These children do not react well to being told what to do. This is not the place to debate whether PDA actually exists as an entity on its own or whether it's a combination of anxiety, mindset etc., nonetheless, the manifestations of the problem exist.

In a workplace most people are given orders; they are told what to do by a supervisor and the expectation is that they will comply with those orders without arguing without pitching a fit and without delay. If you are unable to do those things the odds are you will not keep your job very long.

∾

There are young adults on the autism spectrum who have not and likely never will attend post-secondary school. Can they hold down jobs? Perhaps.

Again, this will depend on their ability level, their attitude, their desire and the training or practice they have received. There are autistic young people who have jobs stocking shelves. For some they might work in large department stores on the night shift. The advantage of this is that there are few or no customers in the store who could interrupt them by asking where things are. They might get to work in a quieter environment and more at their own pace. If they are an exact type of person, they might enjoy lining things up properly on the shelves, putting things in the proper order, and at the end of the shift having completed the tasks that were signed.

I know a young woman who was stocking shelves quite capably during the day and was proud of her efforts. But she would become very frustrated with the customers who would come along and make a mess of her nicely organized shelf. She wanted to tell them to leave things alone and put things back, and to not touch. That was not the job for her.

Being out in the world, rubbing shoulders with other people, and trying to block out the sensory stimuli that might be bombarding them can be very fatiguing. Going home and having some down time can be absolutely crucial. For this reason, some autistic people feel more successful when they have only a part-time job, which allows them more down time.

~

While it might seem that you focus on your student's challenges and "deficits", there are some positives about being autistic than can make someone a great employee. Here are just a few:

•Many autistic people excel at technical skills. Even if they are not seeking a tech-related job, so many types of employment require a high level of technical, computer-related skills.

•The ability of hyper focus can be a wondrous thing. When engaged in a task many autistics can be totally engrossed and dedicated to what they are doing.

•When your child is not doing what you want, you might see this characteristic as stubbornness. But often in adult life, tenacity is a much-needed trait.

•Tenacity and the ability to hyper focus might suit long work hours or flexible work environments when the goal is to complete a task, then have some down time.

•Although the inability to see the forest for the trees can be an impediment sometimes, such attention to detail might be just what an employer is seeking.

•One downside of some work situations is office gossip. Most autistics will have zero interest in this type of socializing and may not pick up on innuendos and undercurrents.

~

In Samantha Craft's blog *Every Day Aspie* she lists these *10 Considerations for the Autistic Workforce*

1.Anxiety

2.Sensory Processing

3.Communication

4.Socializing

5.Misunderstood and Misinterpretations

6.Knowing What to Expect and Order

7.Feedback

8.Over Work/Under Work

9.Silence and Alone Time

10.Processing Spoken and Written Information

~

As for career choices, well that is a huge question. What type of a job the person might seek and enjoy depends on his or her interests and talents?

It might be assumed that some environments are not good for people on the autism spectrum. Many get easily overwhelmed by sensory inputs. To me a busy commercial kitchen would seem like one of the worst environments. They're noisy, they're busy, there's all kinds of movement with people and utensils whizzing around the room. There are smells of all sorts. Workers in a commercial kitchen have to move at a hectic pace which would prove stressful for many, many people. But it is in just such an environment that some autistic adults are finding success such as Chef Tom Dickinson mentioned above. Another example is Chef Chris Fischer.

So, as always with autism, never assume. Let the person be guided by his interests and skills.

∿

So, bottom line. Can your autistic student hold down a job when he's an adult? Likely. That depends on some of the variables we've already discussed here

The biggest failures that I see are when the preparation has not been done. Sometimes just getting the child through the school system can seem like a huge task. And it is, don't let anyone tell you otherwise. With most typical kids they finish school and have within them a desire to move out and begin their life on their own, whether that's in the world of work or attending a postsecondary program. The change does not come easily for those who have autism. While typical kids listen to what their peers are doing and they catch that bug about moving out on their own, that might not happen when a kid is autistic. For one, they might not pick up on the social nuances that say it would not be cool to remain living with your parents. For another thing, that whole moving out business is pretty darn scary.

Think about it. Think of when you first left home. There's the business of finding a place to live getting the money for a down payment or for a damage deposit plus the first month's rent. Then once you're in your own place, what do you do? How do you get furniture? How do you feed yourself? What do you cook on? These things can all be overwhelming for any young person but if you have autism, it can seem insurmountable. So, preparation starts years and years ahead. A decade early is by no means too soon. Start with chores and responsibilities around the house. I don't mean that your eight-year-old should be a slave to housework, but that eight-year-old can certainly contribute. At that age he can do some of the vacuuming he can load or unload the dishwasher, set the table, and many, many other things that he can do to contribute to the well-being of the family. By early teen years most kids can, with assistance, do laundry. The more that a kid has experience with at home the easier it will be for him to manage himself later on.

～

Amanda's videos https://www.youtube.com/watch?v=4c5_3wqZ3Lk&t=287s.

Carly's videos https://www.youtube.com/watch?v=xMBzJleeOno&t=84s.

Common misperceptions about autistic employees https://www.autismspeaks.org/blog/common-misconceptions-about-autistic-employees,

PATHOLOGICAL DEMAND AVOIDANCE

PATHOLOGICAL DEMAND AVOIDANCE

Have you ever had a student who seems resistant? Just plain resistant to anything - to directions you issue, to changing tasks, to going somewhere, even when you know it is something he enjoys. You are likely not imagining things; some kids truly do use resistance as their default mode. Why?

Although it is not an official diagnosis, some people call this Pathological Demand Avoidance[238]. To me, PDA is best understood in terms of anxiety. There are plenty of reasons for autistic kids to be anxious. Here are just a few:

• Their sensory processing differences put them on high alert much of the time,

• they have trouble making sense of the world,

• they don't know what they might encounter or what might be expected of them,

•communication is a challenge for them, both receptive, expressive and nonverbal communication,

•they don't pick up on the social cues that other kids automatically seem to know,

•their natural way of interacting and responding seems at odds with those around them,

•the speed in which they process information may well not match that of those around them,

•their physical skills and ability to do things on command may be weak, compared to their peers.

When you're anxious and have all this going on, might it be your tendency to freeze? Or to rebel against any sort of change when you have just (semi) gotten used to what's happening now?

If you only follow one of the links in this book, please make it this next one. A wonderfully articulate young man explains while he is often resistant to change, what is behind his "demand avoidance", how his anxiety affects his live and the Different Ways of Not Being Able to Do Something[239].

2 [39] https://www.autism.org.uk/about/what-is/pda.aspx.
[240] https://www.youtube.com/watch?v=YKA39DoA10o.

HOW CAN I BE ALL THINGS TO ALL STUDENTS?

ou can't. You just can't, try as you might.

But you can be some things to each and every one of your students. And, that means a lot.

One of the hardest things about teaching is realizing that some of your students have more needs than you can meet. Some of their needs will be out of your control. Although the majority of kids come from loving, caring homes, sadly that is not true for every child who will enter your classroom. These are heartbreaking observations for teachers.

Some of your students will be raised in poverty, where what most of us regard as necessities of life are scarce. It is hard to see a child go hungry. Some schools have breakfast programs and or lunch programs.

Sometimes a teacher will feel strongly that a child should be benefiting from the free or subsidized food given out at school, but the parent has not given permission for the child to participate. It might be a matter of pride. It might mean that the parent does not want anyone else to know of the financial constraints in their home. Maybe the amount of food available at home varies depending on the time of the month, when the last paycheck was received, or if there are addictions in the form of binging.

I know many teachers who purposefully pack themselves huge lunches every day, knowing that they will be sharing their meal with some of their students. Most of us are not familiar with true hunger, but there are times when our stomach rumbles and we may feel that cloying emptiness in our belly or get a little shaky. Think about when that happens. How well do you think? Is your ability to concentrate at its best? How well do you take your new information? How well do you remain focused on a task, especially a task that you do not find fascinating? Now, consider the children in your care who come to your room hungry and how that fact of life might affect their learning.

Autistic kids may come from such homes. You might also have an autistic student who is hungry, but not because he has not been offered food at home. (We'll cover this in the chapter, *What If He Won't Eat at School?*

A teacher has a moral and ethical obligation to report suspected abuse to the authorities. This includes sexual abuse, physical abuse or neglect. It is a hard call for teachers.

What if you are wrong? What if the parent gets mad at you? Worse, what if the parent takes it out on the child? Each state and province has its own policies; you should be familiar with them and what is required if you suspect the possibility that a child in your room is being abused or neglected. In most cases, the onus is not on you to verify whether abuse or neglect is taking place - that is the job of the social workers or police.

This can be even trickier if your student is autistic. Just having an autism diagnosis means that that child is likely even more vulnerable than would be another child of that same age. If the student is nonverbal then it is even harder to get a good handle on what might be going on at home.

Some autistic kids, when they become overwhelmed or

distraught, will harm themselves. This self-abuse might include biting their fingers, hands or arms, hitting themselves, pulling their own hair, head-banging, throwing themselves against walls or objects, etc. Understandably, there could be blood or bruising. How do you know if the bruising has been self-inflicted or if someone is doing that to the child?

Get to know that child. Do you see evidence of him harming himself at school? What have his previous teachers noticed? Does he see a psychologist, speech therapist, occupational therapist, counselor, etc.? Talk to these people about what you are wondering and talk to your school administrator. Depending on your relationship with the parents, and the advice of your administrator, talk to the family about the patterns you see of the child hurting himself at school.

Ask how they handle it at home. What strategies work to calm him when he is out in public or relaxing at home? How do the parents recognize the signs that things are escalating? Which strategies do they put in place to help calm the child before he hurts himself?

Consider the communication and sensory aspects that might overwhelm the child, leading to episodes of stress and self-abuse. Not understanding what is going on, what will happen next or what might be expected of him will increase his anxiety. Not being able to communicate his wants and needs will raise anxiety levels. (Keep in mind that even autistic kids who *can* speak might lose this ability during times of stress). Being assaulted with sensory input will provoke anxiety reactions.

Again, get to know your student. Observe his reactions and responses. Heed his communication and his sensory needs. Occupational therapists and speech/language therapists will be good allies.

Most of all, you want this student (and all students) to feel that you're rooting for them and believe in them. Check out this short article on How to Be an Autistic Ally. [241]

REFERENCES

C hapter 1 - What Is Autism, Anyway?

1 Dr. Damian Milton and monotropism https://www.youtube.com/watch?v=MUDQD1p2zFE.

2 Me and Monotropism https://www.bps.org.uk/psychologist/me-and-monotropism-unified-theory-autism.

3 Sara Harvey's talk on What Is Autism to You? https://www.youtube.com/watch?v=H8hHGIJKf3o&t=99s

4 Diagnostic criteria - Centers for Disease Control https://www.cdc.gov/nchddd/autism/hcp-dsm.html.

5 Diagnostic and criteria exemplars https://depts.washington.edu/dbpeds/Screening%20Tools/DSM-5%28ASD.Guidelines%29Feb2013.pdf

6 It's a Spectrum Doesn't Mean What You Think https://theaspergian.com/2019/05/04/its-a-spectrum-doesnt-mean-what-you-think.

. . .

Chapter 2 - Autistic Student or a Student With Autism?

7 https://www.cdc.gov/ncbddd/disabilityandhealth/materials/factsheets/fs-communicating-with-people.html.

8 https://www.disabilityisnatural.com/people-first-language.html.

9 https://www.youtube.com/watch?v=oFGByJN7I5Y

10 https://autisticadvocacy.org/about-asan/identity-first-language/

11 https://adayinourshoes.com/people-first-language/

12 https://news.northeastern.edu/2018/07/12/unpacking-the-debate-over-person-first-vs-identity-first-language-in-the-autism-community/.

13 https://themighty.com/topic/other-disorder/should-you-use-person-first-or-identity-first-language2/.

14 https://youtu.be/YVPjMfgjmU4.

15 https://youtu.be/oDnQFQFQ8ec.

Chapter 3 - What Caused Him to Have Autism?

16 Autism genetics applied https://www.spectrumnews.org/news/autism-genetics-explained/.

17 Early brain overgrowth Early brain overgrowth https://www.youtube.com/watch?v=k7sYLtq0_F8.

Chapter 4 - Is Autism Something He'll Outgrow?

. . .

1[8] https://www.youtube.com/watch?v=fn_9f5x0f1Q&t=292s.
[19] https://theaspergian.com/2019/04/24/ten-things-we-love-about-being-autistic/.

Chapter 5 - Do I Have to Arrange My Whole Classroom for Him?

2[0] Tips for Teachers: Understanding Students with Autism, from a former student on the Autism Spectrum https://youtu.be/sTh5eGQSsEU

[21] Dos and Don'ts of Classroom Decorations https://www.edutopia.org/article/dos-and-donts-classroom-decorations.

[22] Sensory challengers of students https://network.autism.org.uk/knowledge/insight-opinion/sensory-challenges-autistic-pupils.

[23] 3 Golden Rules for Supporting Autistic Pupils https://www.tes.com/news/three-golden-rules-supporting-autistic-pupils.

[24] Letting Go of Control and Rethinking Support for Autistic Individuals. Compliance is NOT the Goal https://www.uri.edu/tedx/talks/amy-laurent-rethinking-support-for-autistic-individuals.

[25] Human diversity should be celebrated, not treated as a disorder https://youtu.be/aWxmEv7fOFY.

[26] The World Needs All Kinds of Minds https://youtu.be/UKhg68QJlo0.

[27] Normal....Is a Dryer Setting https://www.youtube.com/watch?v=_df8_IlLXog&t=504s.

[28] Make Differences Ordinary in an Inclusive Classroom https://www.academia.edu/1604758/Making_differences_ordinary_in_inclusive_classrooms.

. . .

Chapter 6 - Why is He Not Like Other Autistic Students I've Known?

[8] https://theaspergian.com/2019/06/09/autistic-spectroscopy-spectrum/.

[29] https://theaspergian.com/2019/06/09/autistic-spectroscopy-spectrum/

[30] A Day in the Life of a Slow Processing Child https://www.understood.org/en/learning-attention-issues/child-learning-disabilities/information-processing-issues/a-day-in-the-life-of-a-child-with-slow-processing-speed.

[31] https://www.youtube.com/watch?v=9fUi1EYq6Rs&t=45s.

[32] C.L. Lynch's article https://theaspergian.com/2019/05/04/its-a-spectrum-doesnt-mean-what-you-think/.

Chapter 7 - Which Professionals Might be Involved?

[2] Typical speech and language development https://www.asha.org/public/ speech/development/chart.

[33] What is an occupational therapist? What is Occupational Therapy - Canadian Association of Occupational https://www.caot.ca/site/aboutot/whatisot?nav=sidebar.

[34] On OT working with kids https://youtu.be/rUGLihrh4EI.

Chapter 8 - Is He High or Low Functioning?

. . .

3⁵ Listen to Autistic People www.msn.com/en-us/health/ wellness/this-autism-awareness-month-please-listen-to-autistic-people/ar-BBW3dDD.

³⁶Why Intelligence Scores Do Not Predict Success for Autistic Adults www.spectrumnews.org/opinion/viewpoint/intelligence-scores-not-predict-success-autistic-adults/.

³⁷ What About Functioning drexel.edu/autismoutcomes/blog/ overview/2015/September/What-About-Functioning.

³⁸ Functioning Labels: Why You Shouldn't Be Using Them www.theautisticadvocate.com/2017/10/functioning-labels-why-you-shouldnt-be.html.

Chapter 9 - What If He Doesn't Look At Me?

3⁹ Randrforautism.com.

⁴⁰Reference and Regulate videos http://video. randrforautism.com.

⁴¹ How Autism Affects Eye Contact https://www.youtube.com/ watch?v=zTk76x1RWE4&feature=youtu.be.

⁴²Autism Eye Contact Must Know Info https://www.youtube. com/watch?v=-OH_COVkRUQ&feature=youtu.be.

⁴³ What About Eye Contact? https://www.youtube.com/watch? v=QXM9Mj5Zd7I.

⁶⁴⁴ People with Autism Describe Why Eye Contact Can Be Difficult https://youtu.be/yk7BjvfZjY8.

⁴⁵ You're Not Autistic You Make Eye Contact https://youtu.be/ LI8fQshEEkw.

⁴⁶ Autistic Lack of Eye Contact: Normal Human Behavior https://www.youtube.com/watch?v=WMVhrhXO1Sk.

⁴⁷ Autistic Traits: Eye Contact Avoidance https://www.youtube.

com/watch?v=g5_9XXnv4LY.

[48] http://functionalneurologyminute.com/why-eye-contact-over-stimulates-people-with-autism/.

[49] https://www.sciencedaily.com/releases/2017/06/170615213252.htm.

[50] https://www.sciencealert.com/for-those-with-autism-eye-contact-isn-t-just-weird-it-s-distressing.

[51] https://www.medicinenet.com/script/main/art.asp?articlekey=205085.

[52] https://neurosciencenews.com/eye-contact-autism-6995/.

[53] Autism Eye Contact - Why I Never Ask Autistic Children to Look In My Eyes Why I never ask Autistic children to look in my eyes https://youtu.be/xxqlPXD8yu0.

Chapter 10 - What If He Can't Talk?

[54] Do2Learn Picture Cards http://do2learn.com/picturecards/overview.htm

[55] Symbols for communications https://mulberrysymbols.org.

[56] Autism Goes to School https://Books2Read.com/AutismGoestoSchool.

[57] Social Stories https://carolgraysocialstories.com/social-stories/what-is-it/.

[58] Proloquo2Go https://www.assistiveware.com/products/proloquo2go.

[59] Assistive Communication Apps in the iPad App Store https://www.friendshipcircle.org/blog/2011/02/07/7-assistive-communication-apps-in-the-ipad-app-store

[60] AAC Apps Review https://www.speechandlanguagekids.com/aac-apps-review/.

[61] Cheap, Easy-Use Augmentative Alternative Communication

AAC Devices https://www.speechandlanguagekids.com/cheap-easy-use-augmentative-alternative-communication-aac-devices/.

[62] Free and Inexpensive AAC Apps http://www.centralcoastchildrensfoundation.org/draft/wp-content/uploads/2012/03/FreeandInexpensiveAACAppsFinal.pdf.

[63] Top Alternative and Augmentative Communication https://www.lifewire.com/top-alternative-and-augmentative-communication-198828.

[64] Becca's App Reviews https://www.bluebeepals.com/app-reviews/beccas-app-reviews/free-augmentative-alternative-communication-apps-for-ipad/.

[65] Pictello https://www.assistiveware.com/products/pictello.

[66] Pictello demonstration https://www.youtube.com/watch?v=9B1fAaAS3N4&t=38s.

[67] AAC Will Not Stop a Person From Learning to Speak https://www.assistiveware.com/learn-aac/roadblock-aac-will-stop-a-person-from-learning-to-speak.

[68] AAC Does Not Hinder Natural Speech http://www.rockybay.org.au/wp-content/uploads/2013/04/1.3-AAC-Does-Not-Hinder-Natrual-Speech-Development.pdf

[69] AAC https://www.asha.org/PRPSpecificTopic.aspx?folderid=8589942773&section=Key_Issues.

[70] Effects of AAC Communication on Speech Production on Children with Autism https://pubs.asha.org/doi/10.1044/1058-0360(2008/021).

[71] Dynavox https://www.tobiidynavox.com/en-US/products/devices/.

[72] Nonverbal and presuming competence https://theaspergian.com/2019/07/22/logical-fallacies/.

[73] American Sign Language http://www.lifeprint.com.

[74] British Sign Language www.british-sign.co.uk/what-is-british-sign-language/.

[75] Makaton www.makaton.org/aboutMakaton/.

[76] Baby Sign www.babysignlanguage.com/basics/.

[77] Using Sign Language www.speechandlanguagekids.com/ using-sign-language/.

[78] Apraxia www.asha.org/public/speech/disorders/Childhood-Apraxia-of-Speech/.

[79] Phillip - I Have Nonverbal Autism. Here's What I Want You to Know https://researchautism.org/i-have-nonverbal-autism-heres-what-i-want-you-to-know./

[80] Ido is a nonverbal man continuing his education in college http://idoinautismland.com/?p=843.

[81] Kaylie Clinton - Hear Me Speak Without a Voice http:// kayliespeaks.blogspot.com/2018.

[82] James Potthast - this nonverbal high school graduate writes a blog https://returningjames.com/2018/06/.

[83] Emma - I am an autistic teenager whose body and mouth-words do not always pay attention to my bright and wise mind https://the-art-of-autism.com/emma-an-autistic-girl-whose-body-and-mouth-words-do-not-always-pay-attention-to-her-bright-and-wise-mind/.

[84] Noah - Being nonverbal doesn't mean I can't think https:// monadelahooke.com/being-nonverbal-doesnt-mean-i-cant-think/.

[85] Mike Weinstein was once thought to be intellectually disabled www.goldenhatfoundation.org/about-us/blog/125-golden-hat-foundation-blog-70211.

[86] Carly Fleischmann is nonverbal and has a You Tube channel www.youtube.com/watch?v=xMBzJleeOno&t=164s.

[87] Amanda Baggs talks about being considered retarded www.youtube.com/watch?v=qn70gPukdtY&t=6s.

Chapter 11 - Why Does He Speak Sometimes, But Not At Others?

. . .

.

8 [8] An autistic opinion on echolalia https://www.youtube.com/watch?v=8OeyOMrp68w.

[89] Ask an autistic - what is echolalia https://www.youtube.com/watch?v=ome-95iHtB0&feature=youtu.be.

Chapter 12 - What If He Talks Too Much?

9 [0] Why My Child Talks Non-Stop and What Can I Do? https://www.understood.org/en/learning-attention-issues/child-learning-disabilities/hyperactivity-impulsivity/my-child-talks-nonstop-what-can-i-do.

[91] https://www.youtube.com/watch?v=aoA-CTsBtJM.

[92] https://www.youtube.com/watch?v=2FcXK5UVYXY.

Chapter 13 - Why Is He So Loud Sometimes?

9 [3] Control-O-Meter http://autismteachingstrategies.com/autism-strategies/control-o-meter-social-skills-tool-for-kids-with-autism-helps-with-voice-volume-other-behavior/.

[294] How to Get Children with Autism to Lower Their Voice https://howtoadult.com/children-autism-lower-voice-11626.html.

[95] Get Children with Autism to Lower Their Voice https://www.livestrong.com/article/1001651-children-autism-lower-voice/.

. . .

Chapter 14 - Give Me Just One Strategy I Can Use

⁹⁶ Picture cards https://do2learn.com/picturecards/overview.htm

⁹⁷ Dr. Luke Beardon https://tesnews.podbean.com/e/three-golden-rules-for-supporting-autistic-pupils-tes-podagogy/.

Chapter 15 - What If The Parents Won't Allow Accommodations?

⁹⁸ https://www.specialeducationguide.com/pre-k-12/response-to-intervention/effective-rti-strategies-for-teachers/.

²⁹⁹https://www.rti4success.org.

¹⁰⁰ https://iris.peabody.vanderbilt.edu/resources/iris-resource-locator/.

Chapter 16 - What Is It With This Sensory Stuff?

¹⁰⁰ https://www.youtube.com/watch?v=FhUDyarzqXE.

¹⁰¹https://www.youtube.com/watch?v=49u6rWQ9RgI&feature=youtu.be&list=RDQMq0PM4wH7Vi8.

¹⁰² https://www.understood.org/en/learning-attention-issues/treatments-approaches/therapies/download-sample-sensory-diet.

. . .

Chapter 17 - Tactile Sensory System

[103]Fidget rings and Fidget bands for adults or older students

Chapter 18 - Olfactory Sensory System

[104] https://amzn.to/2YjtS1k.
[105] https://amzn.to/339ua9T.

Chapter 19 - Visual Sensory System

[105] https://youtu.be/bDvKnY0g6e4.
[106] https://www.understood.org/en/school-learning/for-educators/universal-design-for-learning/the-principles-of-universal-design-for-learning.
[107] https://www.understood.org/en/school-learning/assistive-technology/assistive-technologies-basics/video-how-schools-can-use-universal-design-for-learning.
[108] https://udlresource.ca.
[109] https://udlresource.ca.
[110] https://amzn.to/2Yp72p1.
[111] https://www.aap.org/en-us/about-the-aap/aap-press-room/news-features-and-safety-tips/Pages/Children-and-Media-Tips.aspx.

[112] https://www.sleepfoundation.org/articles/how-blue-light-affects-kids-sleep.

Chapter 20 - Auditory Sensory System

[13] https://www.youtube.com/watch?v=KurXpARairU&t=51s.
[114] https://www.youtube.com/watch?v=KurXpARairU&t=51s.
[115] https://www.youtube.com/watch?v=DgDR_gYk_a8&t=19s.
[116] What is Central Auditory Processing Disorder? https://www.youtube.com/watch?v=nW2KsdjYt0k&t=103s.
[117] Picking up directions in a noisy environment https://www.pbs.org/wgbh/misunderstoodminds/experiences/attexp2a.html.

Chapter 21 - Gustatory Sense

[18] https://handsonotrehab.com/gustatory-sensory-system-taste/

Chapter 22 - Vestibular System

[19] Vestibular system https://www.neuroscientificallychallenged.com/blog/know-your-brain-vestibular-system.
[120] Cushion for wobbling https://amzn.to/2YyScN1.
[121] Hokki stool https://amzn.to/2Kq2eap.

[122] One-legged stool https://amzn.to/2KFcZVh.
[123] T-stool https://amzn.to/2YR8bWL.
[124] Standing desk https://amzn.to/2YGJzA5.

Chapter 23 - Proprioceptive Sense

[19] Proprioception http://sensory-processing. middletownautism.com/sensory-strategies/strategies-according-to-sense/proprioceptive.

[120] Pressure vest https://amzn.to/2YALAh7.

[122] Example of a lap weight https://amzn.to/31EiSIZ.

[123] 50 Heavy Work Activities for Kids www.andnextcomesl.com/2015/06/heavy-work-activities-for-kids.html.

[124] Theraband https://amzn.to/2GQUbBl.

[125] Weighted blanket https://amzn.to/2YRiIMN.

[126] How heavy should a weighted product be? www.nationalautismresources.com/weighted-vest-faqs/.

[127] Denim weighted vest https://amzn.to/2Kq4tKR.

[128] Weighted compression vest https://amzn.to/33lGt2N.

[129] Anxiety http://anxietycanada.com/learn-about-anxiety/anxiety-in-children.

Chapter 24 -Interoception

[30] Interoception www.understood.org/en/learning-attention-issues/child-learning-disabilities/sensory-processing-issues/interoception-and-sensory-processing-issues-what-you-need-to-know.

[131] 8 Fun Breathing Exercises for Kids https://childhood101.com/fun-breathing-exercises-for-kids/.

[132] 3 Breathing Exercises to Calm Kids of All Ages www.mother.ly/parenting/3-breathing-exercises-to-calm-kids-of-all-ages.

[133] In Cases of Too Much Interoception https://www.kelly-mahler.com/resources/videos/how-i-feel-episode-4-in-cases-of-too-much-interoception/.

[134] Autism and the One Big Thing No One is Talking about - Interoception. https://www.kelly-mahler.com/resources/videos/interoception-the-new-topic-in-autism/.

[135] Interoception, Neuroscience and Behavior www.youtube.com/watch?v=VU9CqbhmBWQ.

[136] How I Feel - Making Sense of Emotions Through Interoception http://youtu.be/1XJX2MlzTd0.

[137] Interoception: The "Hidden Sense" www.spdstar.org/sites/default/files/file-attachments/Interoception_Info_Sheet_7_17_0.pdf.

Chapter 25 - But I Teach High School. What Does This Have to Do With Me?

[138] https://www.understood.org/en/school-learning/assistive-technology/assistive-technologies-basics/assistive-technology-thats-built-into-mobile-devices.

[139] Amanda Bagg's video on How to Boil Water https://youtu.be/9fUi1EYq6Rs.

[140] LiveScribe pen https://amzn.to/31KJus5.

[141] Video demonstration of LiveScribe pen ShortForm-Generic-480p-16-9-1409173089793-rpcbe5.mp4.

[142] 5 Simple Strategies for Note-Taking https://www.understood.org/en/school-learning/learning-at-home/

homework-study-skills/5-simple-strategies-for-note-taking.
[143] 11 Apps to Help Kids with Note-Taking Issues https://www.
understood.org/en/school-learning/assistive-technology/finding-
an-assistive-technology/11-apps-to-help-kids-with-note-taking.
[144]https://www.spedadulting.com/secondary-sped-follow/.
[145]http://www.opdt-johnson.com/gardner.MI.activites.pdf.

Chapter 26 - What About When Unexpected Things Happen?

[146] Idiom explanation https://youtu.be/OCxgd1OqcYI.
[147] Explaining an idiom https://youtu.be/OCxgd1OqcYI.
[148] What is catastrophizing? https://psychcentral.com/lib/
what-is-catastrophizing/.
[149]https://www.youtube.com/watch?v=91vKS-WrYWI.
[150] https://jillkuzma.files.wordpress.com/2008/09/big-little-
problem-5-point-chart.pdf.

Chapter 27 - Is He Just Lazy?

[151]Sara Harvey - Depression and Inertia - https://www.
youtube.com/watch?v=3StCt1FK4Pc&t=47s.
[152] Autistic inertia www.youtube.com/watch?v=3StCt1FK4Pc&
t=47s.
[153] Fergus Murray - Me and Monotropism https://
thepsychologist.bps.org.uk/me-and-monotropism-unified-theory-
autism.
[154]Mind mapping explanation: https://litemind.com/what-is-
mind-mapping/

AUTISM QUESTIONS TEACHERS ASK

[155]6 free mind mapping tools: https://www.makeuseof.com/tag/8-free-mind-map-tools-best-use/.

[156]MindMup free, online mind mapping tool: https://www.mindmup.com.

[157]Best mind mapping tools of 2023 https://zapier.com/blog/best-mind-mapping-software/

Chapter 28 - What is Stimming?

[159] https://www.andnextcomesl.com/2019/03/autism-stimming.html.

[160] An Autistic Perspective on Stim Suppression https://www.youtube.com/watch?v=jJhcrBHWlDw.

[161] Fergus Murray https://thepsychologist.bps.org.uk/me-and-monotropism-unified-theory-autism.

[162]What is Stimming? https://www.youtube.com/watch?v=WexCWZPJE6A .

[163] Stimming? What's That? https://youtu.be/8bhT2R9HiLs.

[164] Autistic Stimming https://www.youtube.com/watch?v=2vItnXF46gA.

[165] What is Stimming and Why Do Autistic People Stim? https://youtu.be/hPMR7mDSIaI.

[166] Sensory Overload and Why Stimming Helps https://www.youtube.com/watch?v=62wi9_A8vr4.

Chapter 29 - Why is He Always Late?

[167]For people with autism, time is a slippery concept https://www.spectrumnews.org/opinion/for-people-with-autism-time-is-slippery-concept/

· · ·

Chapter 30 - What is Executive Functioning?

168 How Kids Use Executive Function Skills to Learn https://www.understood.org/en/learning-attention-issues/child-learning-disabilities/executive-functioning-issues/how-kids-use-executive-functions-to-learn.

169 Common Myths About Executive Functioning Issues https://www.understood.org/en/learning-attention-issues/child-learning-disabilities/executive-functioning-issues/5-common-myths-about-executive-functioning-issues.

170 Why Kids With Executive Functioning Issues Have Trouble Starting Tasks https://www.understood.org/en/learning-attention-issues/child-learning-disabilities/executive-functioning-issues/why-kids-with-executive-functioning-issues-have-trouble-starting-tasks.

171 Working Memory: What It Is and How It Works https://www.understood.org/en/learning-attention-issues/child-learning-disabilities/executive-functioning-issues/working-memory-what-it-is-and-how-it-works.

172 5 Ways Kids Use Working Memory to Learn https://www.understood.org/en/learning-attention-issues/child-learning-disabilities/executive-functioning-issues/5-ways-kids-use-working-memory-to-learn.

173 A Day in the Life of a Slow Processing Child https://www.understood.org/en/learning-attention-issues/child-learning-disabilities/information-processing-issues/a-day-in-the-life-of-a-child-with-slow-processing-speed.

174 Slow Processing Speed and Anxiety: What You Need to Know https://www.understood.org/en/learning-attention-issues/child-learning-disabilities/information-processing-issues/slow-processing-speed-and-anxiety-what-you-need-to-know.

[175] Slow Processing Speed Fact Sheet https://www.understood. org/en/learning-attention-issues/child-learning-disabilities/ information-processing-issues/slow-processing-speed-fact-sheet.
[176] Can Processing Speed Ever Improve? https://www. understood.org/en/learning-attention-issues/child-learning-disabilities/information-processing-issues/can-processing-speed-ever-improve.
[177] How to Talk to Your Child About Slow Processing https:// www.understood.org/en/learning-attention-issues/ understanding-childs-challenges/talking-with-your-child/how-to-talk-to-your-child-about-slow-processing-speed.
[178] 4 Ways Brain Structure and Chemistry May Affect Processing Speed https://www.understood.org/en/learning-attention-issues/child-learning-disabilities/information-processing-issues/at-a-glance-4-ways-brain-structure-and-chemistry-may-affect-processing-speed.
[179] 7 Ways to Help Kids With Slow Processing Speed Take Notes in Class https://www.understood.org/en/learning-attention-issues/child-learning-disabilities/information-processing-issues/7-ways-to-help-kids-with-slow-processing-speed-take-notes-in-class.
[180] Executive Functioning Issues: What You're Seeing in Your Grade-Schooler https://www.understood.org/en/learning-attention-issues/child-learning-disabilities/executive-functioning-issues/executive-functioning-issues-what-youre-seeing-in-your-grade-schooler.
[181] Executive Functioning Issues: What You're Seeing in Your Middle-Schooler https://www.understood.org/en/learning-attention-issues/child-learning-disabilities/executive-functioning-issues/executive-functioning-issues-what-youre-seeing-in-your-middle-schooler.
[182] Executive Functioning Issues: What You're Seeing in Your High Schooler https://www.understood.org/en/learning-attention-issues/child-learning-disabilities/executive-functioning-

issues/executive-functioning-issues-what-youre-seeing-in-your-high-schooler.

[183] Everyday Challenges for Young People With Executive Function Challenges https://www.understood.org/en/learning-attention-issues/child-learning-disabilities/executive-functioning-issues/everyday-challenges-for-young-adults-with-executive-functioning-issues.

[184] How Executive Functioning Issues Affect Teens and Young Adults in the Workplace https://www.understood.org/en/learning-attention-issues/child-learning-disabilities/executive-functioning-issues/how-executive-functioning-issues-impact-teens-and-young-adults-in-the-workplace.

[185] Everyday Challenges for Young Adults With Executive Functioning Issues https://www.understood.org/en/learning-attention-issues/child-learning-disabilities/executive-functioning-issues/everyday-challenges-for-young-adults-with-executive-functioning-issues.

[186] Marshmallow Test https://www.understood.org/en/learning-attention-issues/child-learning-disabilities/executive-functioning-issues/video-the-marshmallow-test-in-action.

[187] Marshmallow Test https://www.understood.org/en/learning-attention-issues/child-learning-disabilities/executive-functioning-issues/video-the-marshmallow-test-in-action.

[188] A Day in the Life of a Child with Executive Functioning Issues https://www.understood.org/en/learning-attention-issues/child-learning-disabilities/executive-functioning-issues/a-day-in-the-life-of-a-child-with-executive-functioning-issues.

[189] 4 Ways Executive Functioning Issues Can Affect Your Child's Social Life https://www.understood.org/en/learning-attention-issues/child-learning-disabilities/executive-functioning-issues/trouble-with-sequencing-what-you-need-to-know.

[190] Very Grand Emotions: How Autistics and Neurotypicals Experience Emotions Differently https://theaspergian.com/2019/03/23/very-grand-emotions/.

[191] https://www.understood.org/en/learning-attention-issues/child-learning-disabilities/executive-functioning-issues/5-ways-executive-functioning-issues-can-impact-reading.

[192] Why Kids With Executive Functioning Issues Have Trouble Planning https://www.understood.org/en/learning-attention-issues/child-learning-disabilities/executive-functioning-issues/why-kids-with-executive-functioning-issues-have-trouble-with-planning.

[193] 10 Tips to Help Your Child Follow Directions https://www.understood.org/en/learning-attention-issues/understanding-childs-challenges/talking-with-your-child/10-tips-to-help-your-child-follow-directions.

[194] How Does the Child with Executive Function Issues Think Differently? https://www.understood.org/en/learning-attention-issues/child-learning-disabilities/executive-functioning-issues/how-does-a-child-with-executive-functioning-issues-think-differently.

[195] Is the Messy Backpack Due to Executive Functioning or Motivation Issues? https://www.understood.org/en/learning-attention-issues/child-learning-disabilities/executive-functioning-issues/is-the-messy-backpack-due-to-executive-functioning-or-motivation-issues.

[196] Executive Functioning Issues and Learning: 6 Ways to Help Your High Schooler https://www.understood.org/en/learning-attention-issues/child-learning-disabilities/executive-functioning-issues/executive-functioning-issues-and-learning-6-ways-to-help-your-high-schooler.

[197] Assistive Technology That's Built into Mobile Devices https://www.understood.org/en/school-learning/assistive-technology/assistive-technologies-basics/assistive-technology-thats-built-into-mobile-devices.

[198] An Inside Look at Executive Functioning Issues https://youtu.be/9qUpgTuMHNQ.

[199] An Autistic Perspective on Autism and Executive

Functioning https://youtu.be/9XH_8hTwlEU.

[200] Ask an Autistic: What is Executive Functioning? https://youtu.be/229Xb50_o8M.

[201] How Autistic People Can Achieve More in Their Life https://youtu.be/1GY54vdtT78.

[202] Developing Executive Function: What Happens in the Brain https://youtu.be/pp_67E25Q7w.

[203] Executive Functioning Issues and Possible Causes https://www.understood.org/en/learning-attention-issues/child-learning-disabilities/executive-functioning-issues/executive-functioning-issues-possible-causes.

[204] Types of Tests for Executive Functioning Issues https://www.understood.org/en/school-learning/evaluations/types-of-tests/tests-for-executive-functioning-issues.

[205] Free e-book on Executive Function 101 https://www.understood.org/en/learning-attention-issues/child-learning-disabilities/executive-functioning-issues/ebook-executive-function-101.

Chapter 31 - How Can I Help Him Be Less Messy?

[206] Is That Messy Backpack Due to Executive Functioning or Motivational Issues? https://www.understood.org/en/learning-attention-issues/child-learning-disabilities/executive-functioning-issues/is-the-messy-backpack-due-to-executive-functioning-or-motivation-issues.

[207] Organizing a student's desk https://youtu.be/nO4KEURDDOQ.

[208] Organizational Tips for Messy Student Desks https://www.thoughtco.com/organizational-tips-for-messy-student-desks-2080981.

[209] How to Organize Your School Desk https://www.wikihow.com/Organize-Your-School-Desk.

[210] Pencil grips for kids https://youtu.be/KVf51TojK1U.

[211] Pencil grips https://amzn.to/2MS0R5T.

[212] How Various Learning and Attention Issues Can Cause Trouble with Handwriting https://www.understood.org/en/learning-attention-issues/child-learning-disabilities/writing-issues/how-various-learning-and-attention-issues-can-cause-trouble-with-writing.

[213] Autism Spectrum Disorder and the Cerebellum https://www.ncbi.nlm.nih.gov/pubmed/24290381.

[214] How is the Cerebellum Linked to Autism Spectrum Disorders? https://www.psychologytoday.com/ca/blog/the-athletes-way/201309/how-is-the-cerebellum-linked-autism-spectrum-disorders.

[215] A Role for the Cerebellum in Autism http://www.hussmanautism.org/cerebellum-review/.

[216] The Cerebellum, Autism and How the Human Brain Gets Organized https://www.youtube.com/watch?v=KwROqh9sOwg.

[217] Autism Spectrum Disorder Linked to the Shape of the Cerebellum https://medicalxpress.com/news/2018-07-autism-spectrum-disorder-linked-brain.html.

Chapter 32 - What If He Won't Eat at School?

Chapter 33 - Why Does He Remind Me of a Student with ADHD?

. . .

[2][18] Attention and monotropism https://journals.sagepub.com/doi/abs/10.1177/1362361305051398.

[219] Monotropism and flow states https://www.youtube.com/watch?v=MUDQD1p2zFE.

[220] Me and Monotropism https://www.bps.org.uk/psychologist/me-and-monotropism-unified-theory-autism.

Chapter 34 - Why is His Hygiene Poor?

[2][21] Autism and Hygiene: Sensory Overload http://youtu.be/sJIiZhDdkO4.

[222] Personal Hygiene www.adders.org/socialstories5.htm.

[223] Personal Hygiene Social Story www.youtube.com/watch?v=fsT3sEjtdME.

[224] How to Take a Shower www.youtube.com/watch?v=dcCVfaLkzJk.

Chapter 35 - How Do I Explain to His Classmates?

[2][25] How Easy Is It to Read the Minds of People with Autism Spectrum Disorder? https://link.springer.com/article/10.1007%2Fs10803-015-2662-8.

[226] Double Empathy Problem by Damian Milton https://www.autism.org.uk/advice-and-guidance/professional-practice/double-empathy.

[227] What is alexithymia? https://www.youtube.com/watch?v=Fl-aKRdzLyQ.

[228] Sara's views on theory of mind and understanding emotions

https://www.youtube.com/watch?v=oj2M9CxBCLc.

[229] Dr. Todd Grande's explanation of alexithymia https://www.youtube.com/watch?v=RsxoV_3QKkc.

Chapter 36 - What Will Happen to Him When He Finishes School?

[230] Stephen Shore https://www.youtube.com/watch?v=0teFbz4TB-A.

[231] Carly Fleischmann https://www.chatelaine.com/living/real-life-stories/my-daughters-severe-autism-and-how-she-found-her-voice/.

[232] Amanda Baggs https://well.blogs.nytimes.com/2008/02/28/the-language-of-autism/..

[233] Klin, Volkmar & Sparrow. Asperger Syndrome (2002), p. 8.

Chapter 37 - Will He Ever Hold Down a Job?

[234] Amanda Bagg's videos https://www.youtube.com/watch?v=4c5_3wqZ3Lk&t=287s.

[235] Carly Fleischmann video https://www.youtube.com/@speechlesswithcarlyfleisch2331.

[236] Chef Tom Dickinson https://youtu.be/GTnjKv32wj4.

[237] Why is the Autistic Unemployment Rate So High? http://www.thinkingautismguide.com/2018/02/why-is-autistic-unemployment-rate-so.html.

[238] What is PDA? https://www.autism.org.uk/about/what-is/pda.aspx.

. . .

Chapter 38 - Pathological Demand Avoidance

2 [39] https://www.autism.org.uk/about/what-is/pda.aspx.
[240] https://www.youtube.com/watch?v=YKA39DoA10o.

Chapter 39 - How Can I Possibly Be All Things to All Students?

2 [41] How to be an Autistic Ally https://youtu.be/JsllOQeWqNg.

SCHOOL DAZE SERIES

Autism Goes to School
Autism Runs Away
Autism Belongs
Autism Talks and Talks
Autism Grows Up
Autism Goes to College

Autism Questions Parents Ask & The Answers They Seek
Autism Questions Teachers Ask & The Answers They Seek

Anything For Her Son (free short story)

SYNOPSIS OF BOOKS IN THE SCHOOL DAZE SERIES

*A*utism Goes to School

After suddenly receiving custody of his five year old son, Ben must learn how to be a dad. The fact that he'd even fathered a child was news to him. Not only does this mean restructuring his sixty-hour workweek and becoming responsible for another human being, but also Kyle has autism.

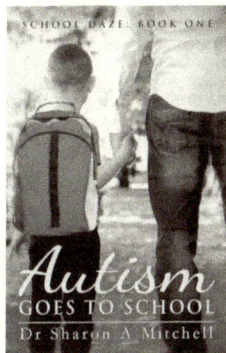

Enter the school system and a shaky beginning. Under the guidance of a gifted teacher, Ben and Kyle take tentative steps to becoming father and son.

Teacher Melanie Nicols sees Ben as a deadbeat dad, but grudgingly comes to admire how he hangs in, determined to learn for his son's sake. Her admiration grows to more as father and son come to rely on Melanie being a part of their lives.

When parents receive the news that their child has autism, they spend countless hours researching the subject, usually at night, after an exhausting day. Teachers, when they hear that they'll have a student with an autism spectrum disorder, also try to learn as much as they can. This award-winning, bestselling novel was written for such parents and teachers - an entertaining read that's fun, yet still offers strategies and information on autism.

～

Autism Runs Away

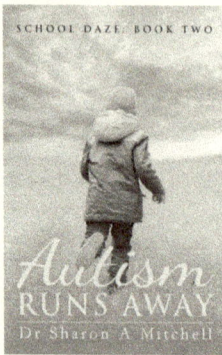

Ethan is only in grade one and already has been *kicked out of one school* due to his tantrums and pattern of running away when in a panic. Now, his mom has enrolled him in a new school but remains glued to her phone, waiting for the call to tell her to come pick him up, that they can't handle him, that they don't know what to do with a child who has **autism**.

How can she trust these strangers to look after her son, just one small child among hundreds, when he has run from own parents so very many times? They don't know the terror of losing your child in a mall or watching him run blindly into traffic.

What started as a fun chase game when Ethan was a toddler has turned into a terrifying deviation. The adults in his life never know when he might take off.

Sara is about to learn if this new school is up to the challenge.

Meet Kyle, Mel, Ben and the other characters you got to know in the award-winning bestseller *Autism Goes to School*. See what they've been up to in the last year and how they join forces to help Ethan.

Then, return to Madson School to see if Manny, a child with severe autism belongs in their midst. Read Manny's story in *Autism Belongs*.

∾

Autism Belongs

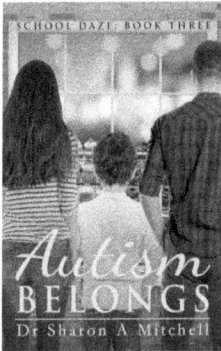

Manny is not like other children. He doesn't talk. He doesn't leave the house. His parents desperately try to arrange their world so that Manny does not get upset. Because, when he does, well, the aggression was getting worse. Too many times Tomas had to leave work to rescue his wife from the havoc of their son's meltdowns. At ten, Manny was becoming difficult to handle.

Dare they consider letting him go to school? Is there a chance that Manny actually **belongs** here? You bet.

Meet Kyle, Ben, Mel and the other characters you read about in the award-winning bestseller *Autism Goes to School* and see how they've grown and progressed.

∾

AUTISM TALKS AND TALKS

Karen is bright, vivacious and highly verbal. Perhaps too verbal. She finds certain topics fascinating and goes on and on and on not realizing she has bored her audience. She remains on the fringe, looking at other adolescents having fun together and wondering if she could ever be a part of the group. Karen has **Asperger's Syndrome**.

Who best to help her but an **autistic chef**. *What?!*

Yep! Meet Jeff. His special talents and view of the world are just

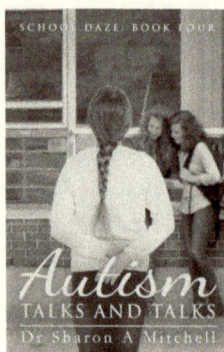

what Karen needs. And, Jeff learns that he is just what one particular woman needs as well.

Is this all there is for Karen? Will an autistic man find the love he didn't know he was seeking? Come join us and see.

~

AUTISM GROWS UP

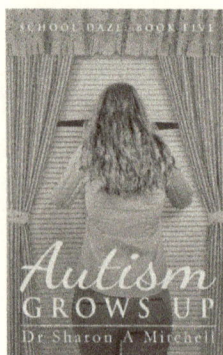

At twenty-one, Suzie has withdrawn from a world she finds alien and confusing. She has Asperger's Syndrome as well as high anxiety. To her, the world is a harsh, scary place where she does not fit.

She spends much of her days sleeping and most of her nights on the computer. Her mother, Amanda, wishes Suzie would get a job, go to school or at least help out around the house. Suzie feels that her time is amply filled with the compelling world lurking within her computer.

Suzie is most content when alone in the basement with her computer. Staring at her monitor, the rest of the world falls away and she feels at home.

What will become of Suzie if something happens to Amanda? But when an intruder breaks into the house, Amanda has only Suzie to rely on.

~

A *UTISM GOES TO COLLEGE*

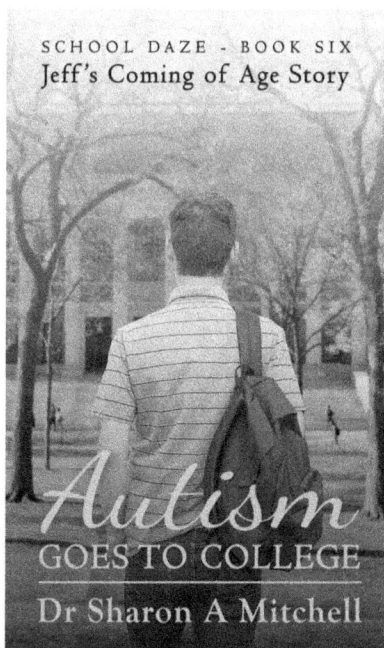

SCHOOL DAZE - BOOK SIX
Jeff's Coming of Age Story

Autism
GOES TO COLLEGE
Dr Sharon A Mitchell

Autism and college. A perfect match or a perfect storm?

An autistic young man emerges from his parents' basement to move away to college. Will it be the life he dreamed of, or his worst nightmare?

This is a coming of age story with a twist. Jeff faces challenges unlike those of typical students. His loving home was a safe haven after years of bullying at school.

His basement refuge provided protection from a harsh and confusing world. Was he prepared to take on that same world now?

If you like relatable characters, real-life situations, and overcoming adversity, then you will love Dr. Mitchell's sixth book in the Autism School Daze series. *Autism Goes to College*

DR. SHARON A. MITCHELL

Autism Goes to School
Autism Runs Away
Autism Belongs
Autism Talks and Talks
Autism Grows Up
Autism Box Set
Autism Goes to College
Autism Questions Parents Ask & Answers They Need
Autism Questions Teachers Ask & Answers They Need

~

I nterested in taking a look at sample chapters from any of these? Contact the author at sharon@ sharonmitchellauthor.com.

~

WHEN BAD THINGS HAPPEN SERIES

BOOKS IN THE SERIES

Psychological thriller series
When Bad Things Happen
Gone
Trust
Selfish
Instinct
Reasons Why
Mine
Sanctum
When a Plan Comes Together
Young Anna (free download at https://dl.bookfunnel.com/
xrj0h5wef9)

G ONE
A sheltered mother. A medically fragile child.
They can't just vanish. But they did.
A typical day of medical appointments and errands. Elizabeth
can handle it, she tells herself. She'll do it

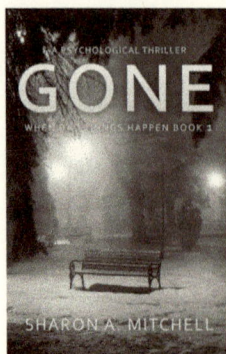

all until her husband returns on the weekend.

But someone else has a plan – several someones, throwing Elizabeth's orderly life into chaos and danger.

Now, she's on her own. No one knows where they are. If her son is to get out of this alive, it's up to Elizabeth.

Ordinary people, thrown into extraordinary circumstances. Read Gone, Book One of the psychological thriller series When Bad Things Happen.

~

TRUST

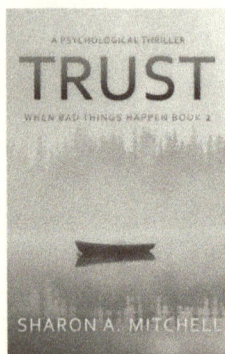

Elizabeth thought that after all they'd been through, the bad parts were over.

Guess not.

After saving herself and her little boy from abductors, Elizabeth yearns to put the terror behind them, to cocoon with her son, safe and secure at home.

Court hearings confirm that they suffered the worst betrayal possible. She never dreamed that she'd have to battle the law to protect her medically fragile little boy when his life and sanity are on the line.

When her son is targeted and taken, Elizabeth will do anything to save him.

Ordinary people, thrust into extraordinary circumstances.

Read *TRUST*, Book Two of the psychological thriller series When Bad Things Happen.

≈

SELFISH

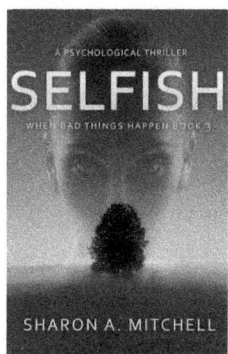

When is being selfish the right thing to do?

A child wanders the courthouse hallways alone. She won't speak. Or, can't speak.

Anna agrees to foster the abandoned girl.

But danger lurks in Anna's past. Just when she thinks that all her striving has finally brought her the life she sought, the past launches itself at her and those she's come to love. Yet other forces are after the child.

With lives and freedom on the line, can Anna shake the bonds on the past, and stand up for those who mean the world to her?

Read *SELFISH*: A Psychological Thriller, Book 3 in the series When Bad Things Happen.

≈

INSTINCT

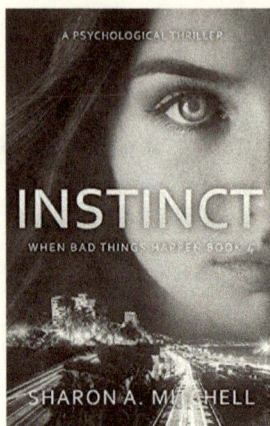

Meet Natalie. She was supposed to take *care* of the child, not *take* the child.

Meet Cynthia. Her husband's life came to an end. She's coming to terms with that loss.

Now the money in her bank account is also coming to an end.

This was not the life she planned, but their little girl depends on her.

After years away, dipping her toe back into her former career is tricky. But it should be doable, right?

Sure, if not for kidnapping, abduction, trafficking, and….

Ignore your instincts at your peril!

Read *INSTINCT*, book 4 in the psychological thriller series When Bad Things Happen.

~

R EASONS WHY
She sold her kids to make a better life for herself.

Sally made choices - choices you might not agree with, like sacrificing her kids. But what if she truly believed that was the best thing for her daughter and sons?

The Sally on the book cover has

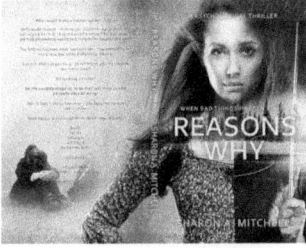

two sides – one warmed by the sun's rays, the other buffeted by storms.

Doesn't that happen to all of us? Which side dominates our world view?

Do we have a choice?

Do life's events shape us, or do they just show us who we really were all along?

This is Sally's story. See what made Sally the woman she is today.

Read Book 5 in the series When Bad Things Happen.

❧

M*INE*

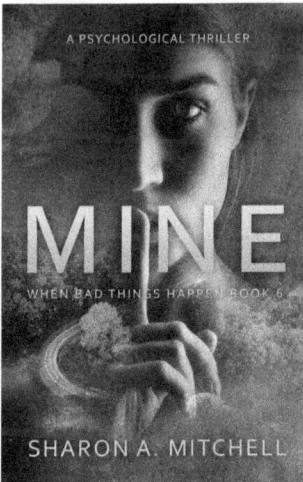

It had always been just Keira and her little boy, Daniel. There was no choice; the father deserted them and her parents disowned her for being pregnant and unmarried.

Now the sperm donor is back and he wants their son. *Needs* their son, he says, and won't go away without him.

Read *MINE*, book 6 in the series When Bad Things Happen.

. . .

SANCTUM

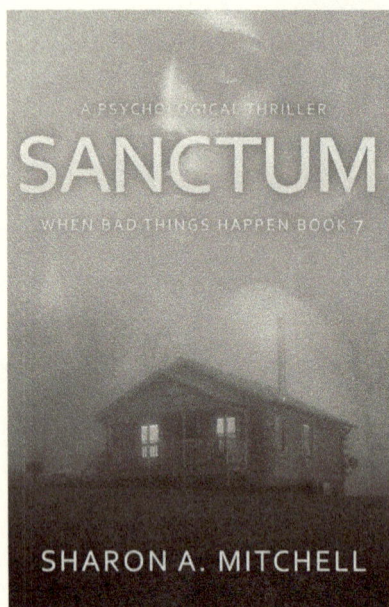

A life beyond redemption.

Wait! That's wrong. Everyone can be redeemed. Right?

Alejandro needed to feel safe, needed to prove to himself he was worth more than trash left at the side of the road.

He did things he felt he needed to do to make it in life. Like a snowball, each event built on the one before, until the nastiness lodged in his soul.

Then his daughter came into his life.

For her sake, can he change? Is that even possible?

❧

ANYTHING FOR HER SON

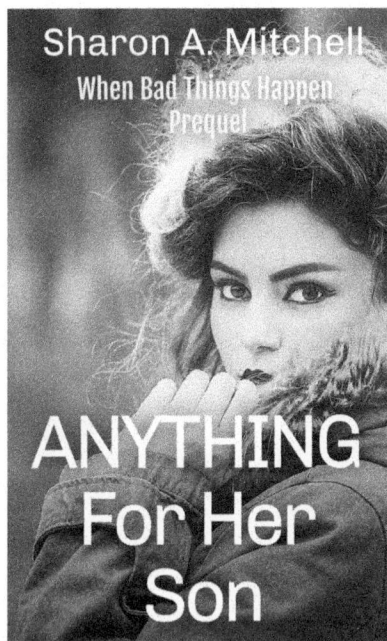

(Get your free download at https://dl.bookfunnel.com/ a27d9uzou0)

I t was just Keira and her little boy, alone against the world. Everyone else had disappointed and deserted them.

Jake Dean is a cop; his mission is to serve and protect. With Keira and Daniel, he'd like to do this and more.

With her worst fears realized, can Keira let down the barriers and allow someone in? It's a matter of trust.

This free short story is a prequel to the series, When Bad Things Happen.

Autism Goes to School
Autism Runs Away
Autism Belongs

DR. SHARON A. MITCHELL

Autism Talks and Talks
Autism Grows Up
Autism Goes to College - Jeff's Coming of Age Story
Autism Questions Parents Ask
Autism Questions Teachers Ask
Free short stories:
Anything for Her Son
Young Anna
Psychological Thriller Series When Bad Things Happen:
Gone
Trust
Selfish
Instinct
Reasons Why
Mine
Sanctum

A PSYCHOLOGICAL THRILLER

GONE

WHEN BAD THINGS HAPPEN BOOK 1

SHARON A. MITCHELL

GONE: A PSYCHOLOGICAL THRILLER PREVIEW

CHAPTERS 1 - 3

PART I
MONDAY

CHAPTER 1

J ackson sipped his morning coffee - just the temperature he liked it, creamy and the best coffee beans Gevalia offered. At least Elizabeth got that right. He turned the newspaper to the next page. Behind his paper screen was the murmur of his wife's voice. You'd almost think she was there alone.

Well, time to get moving. He had stuff to do, a life to get on with and plans to make things even better. He let the paper flop onto his plate of congealing eggs. Straightening his suit, he stood and checked that his cuff links were properly seated.

Elizabeth placed a kiss on their son's forehead and rubbed noses with him. Four-year-old Timothy remained focused on plucking Cheerios off his highchair table.

Irked, Jackson thought he'd try once again. "Isn't he a little old to still be using a highchair? For God's sake, he's almost ready for school and could sit in a chair."

Elizabeth looked up, frowning. "I've explained before. He's much safer strapped into his highchair. He could fall off a chair and get hurt."

Jackson sighed. Turning, he picked up his briefcase in one hand and his suitcase in the other. That was another thing Elizabeth did right - she always had his case packed with exactly the items he'd need to wear during the week.

Elizabeth came to the doorway. She adjusted her husband's tie and brushed the lapels of his suit. Perfect, as always. She looked up at him. "Are you sure you can't come to the neurologist appointment with us this morning?"

"We've been through this. I have to work, you know that. Someone has to pay the bills and keep a roof over our heads." He didn't meet her eyes. "Besides, it'll be the same old, same old anyway."

"But things have changed. They're getting worse."

Of course they are, Jackson thought. And if you wouldn't baby him so much, he'd have a chance of being normal. He glanced over at his son who was oblivious to their conversation, the tension in the air or their very presence, he thought. "Anyway, gotta go." He leaned toward Elizabeth to place the obligatory peck on her cheek.

Behind Elizabeth, a bumping and rattling started as the highchair legs skittered across the floor. She rushed over to their son, wrapping her arms around his head. "He's having a seizure!"

Well again, of course he is, Jackson said to himself. When does he not? He loved his son, he really did, but for just a little while he'd like to have a normal boy, a boy he could play with, take places and be proud of. He shook his head. He was proud of his son, an appealing tike. When out in public, people commented on how good looking he was, but when they tried to engage him, Timothy's eyes slid away. Elizabeth would step in to explain their son's lack of interest, saying he was ill and not feeling well. Partially true; he was ill. That was just it. This was not what Jackson had signed on for. Still, the kid would probably be better if his mother would stop this over-protective bit. Every guy knew that when a baby entered your life, the mom's focus would be on the child for a while. Understandable. But should that baby remain the center of her universe for four whole years, with no end in sight?

He watched a few moments longer as the highchair shook with the violence of Timothy's spasms. Then the odor of urine filled the kitchen. Figures. Kid pissed himself again. If he would not be toilet-trained, he wished Elizabeth would keep the kid's diaper on. At least when he was home, rather than going through this farce of toilet training. He shook his head and went out the door. Outside, he said to the air, "Be back Friday night. See you then." Or not.

～

Elizabeth cradled Timothy's head, protecting it from bruising and bumps on the back and arms of the highchair. Although the seizures rarely lasted more than a minute or so, they could seem to take forever when you held your writhing child in your arms, praying for it to be over, praying for him to be undamaged by this assault on his brain.

Finally, the thrashing stopped, and Timothy slumped to the side. The seizures took so much out of him. He'd sleep for the next hour, at least, and awaken groggy and disoriented. She liked to remain near, providing comfort and whatever security she could offer.

Unstrapping him from the highchair took a while because of the five-point harness and double locking system. Once, before all that was in place, a seizure had thrown him right out of the chair, adding a minor concussion on top of all his other problems.

With her nose that close, Elizabeth could smell the urine. Looking under the chair, she saw the puddle forming. She grimaced, knowing how much Jackson hated that. Well, so did she, and she was sure Timothy felt the same way. It was just that he had no control. None of them had control over this. Timothy actually smiled at her when she dressed him in his big boy underwear this morning. Was it just half an hour ago? She cherished moments like that, when he would look right at her and share his enjoyment. Even if he didn't say it, she knew he was proud to have that diaper off. So much for today's toilet training session.

Lifting a limp forty-pound child out of a snug-fitting highchair was no simple task, but Elizabeth honed this skill over the many times she had to do this on her own. Getting him into her arms, she felt the wet soaking into the sleeve of her new blouse. Another one for the dry cleaners.

She glanced up at the doorway toward her husband. Gone. Out of habit, she schooled her expression so her disappointment wouldn't show, then remembered that there was no one there to pretend for. Jackson was gone; Timothy was sleeping the sleep of the unconscious, as he always did after a major seizure.

It was Monday and Jackson was gone. Another long week of basically single parenting until Jackson returned home Friday.

CHAPTER 2

D r. Muller's office was familiar, sadly familiar. What Elizabeth wouldn't give to have never had reason to enter such a place. Or even if this visit was a one-shot deal. Or their last visit.

Set up for kids, there was a section in the corner with a low wall separating the waiting room chairs from the kids' play area. Meant to be easily climbable by the average child, a startling number of the small kids entering this office needed to be lifted over the barrier to sit in the ball pit or helped to reach for the toys. While some young patients obviously wanted their parents' help in getting to the play area, Timothy showed no such reaction. He appeared neutral to his surroundings, neither clinging to his mom, burying his head against her legs nor clambering to go play. Elizabeth assumed that he was more mature than other preschoolers, already above such things as a ball pit, and so self-possessed that he was content with his own thoughts. At least this meant he wouldn't be one of those kids who screamed when lifted away from the toys to have their turn with the doctor.

Instead, Timothy sat quietly beside his mother, playing with his hands. Jazz hands, she called them; he could twist them into such intriguing shapes and seemed content to do this for hours. Thankfully, Elizabeth thought that he had fewer seizures when quietly occupied. Maybe.

∾

The receptionist called Timothy's name. In the doorway to the hall stood a smiling Dr. Muller. Elizabeth stood, said her son's name softly. When there was no response, she gently took his upper arm and guided him off his chair toward the physician. Dr. Muller squatted to be closer to Timothy's height and held out his hand. "Hi, Timmy. It's good to see you again."

"Timothy," reminded Elizabeth. "His name is Timothy." She gave a soft nudge to her son's shoulder, hoping he would respond to the extended hand. She had practiced this with Timothy at home. While he would shake hands with her, he could not seem to generalize that action with anyone else.

The doctor straightened, unrebuffed and led the way to his office.

∾

"So, how has it been going, young man?" Dr. Muller directed his question to Timothy.

As always, his mom answered for him. "Not well, not well at all."

The neurologist tried again with Timothy. He called his name, waited then called again, watching for a shift in Timothy's attention, a glance his way or some recognition that he had heard his name called. Nothing.

"He's never comfortable in any place but home," Elizabeth explained. Then she started to describe that morning's seizure.

"Wait." Dr. Muller held up his hand. "I'll get the nurse in here to take Timothy away to play. Then we can talk."

"Oh, he won't go with anyone but me."

"I'd prefer not to talk about your son in front of him. If we had some privacy, you can speak more freely."

"That's not a problem. Timothy doesn't talk."

"I'm aware of that. But that doesn't mean that he isn't listening and understanding what we say."

"I only wish that were true. My husband and I talk all the time, and about our concerns over him and he never pays any attention."

"As you wish, Mrs. Whitmore. You are his guardian."

"Yes. As I was saying, the seizures are worse."

"Frequency? Intensity?" he asked.

"Yes, to both. And they're not just absence seizures, or at least we don't notice many of those anymore. Maybe they're still happening, but the major ones take up our attention. Remember those he used to have, the kind where his upper body would stiffen when he was lying down, and he'd sit up?"

"Jackknifing. Are those occurring more now?"

"They do, but it's not just those. Sometimes one arm will rise in the air, straight up, and stay that way for maybe half a minute. You can't bend his arm down when that's happening. He's clunked both Jackson and I in the face several times. At first Jackson got mad, thinking Timothy was doing it on purpose to be funny. But he's not - I swear he is not."

"How often is this happening?"

"Several times a day. And that's not all. Over the last week or two, he's having tonic-clonic seizures. I looked it up on the internet. He seems to lose consciousness, then his body is twitching and moving. If I don't protect him, he hits his head. Hard. I try to keep him by me at all times, because he just drops to the ground when it happens. Once he got this huge bump on his forehead." She brushed Timothy's bangs back, showing the remnants of what was a nasty contusion. "What I need to know is when this will end."

Dr. Muller leaned back in his chair. "I know this isn't what you want to hear, but the honest answer is that I don't know. There's a chance never."

Elizabeth's body moved to the edge of her chair. "But before you called this Infantile Spasms. He's not an infant anymore. I thought that most kids grew out of this."

"West Syndrome," he began.

"But Jackson told me it wasn't West Syndrome."

"Mr. Whitmore did not want it to be West Syndrome." He sighed. "West Syndrome, although we sometimes don't know why it occurs, is a genetic disorder passed down from men to their sons."

"Jackson did not have seizures. Ever. I asked his mother."

"It can be recessive in a man, but still passed on to his son."

"That would mean…".

"Yes, I'm afraid that that's how your husband saw it, that if Timothy had West Syndrome, then the fault or blame lay with the father. There is no blame; it sometimes just happens."

"This is something babies get. I think we first noticed it when Timothy was about six-months-old. It's been three and a half years. Shouldn't he be growing out of it by now? It's getting worse and the seizures are changing."

"I understand. Since he first started having them, we've noticed abnormal EEG patterns. They were consistent with what we often see in West Syndrome. But they do seem to be changing. I think he might be developing a different variety of seizure disorder."

"Okay, that might be good, one you can do something about."

Dr. Muller shook his head. "I'm afraid that what we might be seeing is Lennox Gastaut. It's a rare form of epilepsy that begins in childhood."

"When does it go away?"

"It doesn't, or at least it rarely goes away."

"We can treat it, can't we?"

"We have medications that can help to keep it under some degree of control."

"He's already on anti-epileptic meds!"

"Yes, and he'll remain on some, but we'll tweak the doses, the timing and the exact meds until we find the optimum level of control with as few side effects as possible."

"Side effects?"

"We'll aim for a balance between dampening down the seizure action without overly sedating Timmy."

"Timothy." Elizabeth's voice rose. "It's Timothy. If we had wanted him called Timmy or Tim or some other variation, we would have named him that. We chose Timothy. It's a strong and solid name."

"Sorry." Dr. Muller glanced at the child. "Timothy, I didn't mean to get your name wrong."

The child seemed not to care either way. He fixated on the play of his hands in the sunbeam coming through the south-facing window.

～

Elizabeth took a minute to absorb this news before composing herself. She grasped her son's hands, pulling them tightly to her lap. "What about his development? There was some question about that when you thought it was Infantile Spasms."

"You're right. There is often some degree of cognitive impairment with IS. But, when the child was meeting all development milestones previous to the onset of the seizures, there is a greater chance of development closer to typical."

"Closer." Elizabeth held on to that word. It meant good things. Sort of. "He seems fine now. I mean, just look at what he can do with his hands. He has more dexterity than do kids a year older than him. He can pick up the tiniest speck that I can hardly even see. But he knows it's there and goes after it."

Dr. Muller nodded.

"And he's far more content than most four-year-olds. He hardly needs any entertaining; he can amuse himself for long stretches where other kids plague their parents."

Again, Dr. Muller nodded, encouraging Elizabeth to continue. When she didn't, he asked the one question she did not want to discuss. "How is his speech?"

She looked away. "It's not there. Or, hardly at all."

"Hardly? That you would say that is encouraging. What words does he say? Momma? Daddy? Please? Me? Does he respond to his name? Go get the item you ask for?"

"No, none of those. Not once that we've ever heard. But when he says something, he can go on and on for sentences." Her voice became more enthused. "He can recite long speeches from some of his videos. He loves them and watches them over and over. And he's so smart he can run our DVD player all by himself. And he can find the things he wants to watch from You Tube on the iPad".

They both watched Timothy wave and contort his hands in the air, smiling as he did so.

"He's a beautiful child," Elizabeth whispered.

"Yes, he is a good-looking boy. Mrs. Whitmore, I wonder if there is something else we're seeing here."

"This Lennox-Gastaut?"

"Well, that and possibly something else as well."

"Something you can cure? Something that will go away?"

"I'm afraid not. We are likely talking about a lifelong condition. Conditions, to be exact."

∾

E lizabeth pushed back her chair and reached for her son. She swept him into her arms. "Thank you, Dr. Muller. Anything further will have to wait until my husband is with us. He was really not pleased about the possibility of West Syndrome, and I doubt he will like the sounds of what you are insinuating now." She took several steps toward the door. "We'll call to make an appointment when Jackson can be here."

"Just a minute, please." Dr. Muller held up a piece of paper. "Here are your prescriptions for the new medications. You remember how we weaned him gradually off the current medication by going from three times a day to two, then one, then giving one day of rest before beginning the new one. The valproic acid waChapters not giving as much control as we'd like, so we'll see what a combination of Lamictal and Clobazam will do. Begin with the Lamictal first, just one before bed then by this weekend, add one Clobazam first thing in the morning. We'll see what that does."

"We'll see? Aren't you supposed to *know*?"

"I wish I did, but medicine is not an exact science. Everyone's metabolism handles compounds differently. We'll need to play around with this until we find the best combination to give him some relief."

Clutching her son tightly, Elizabeth fled, prescriptions in hand.

Behind her, the receptionist called. "Mrs. Whitmore, don't you want to make your next appointment? Dr. Muller said he wanted to see you in two weeks."

"Later. I'll call you later when I know my husband's schedule. I want him here the next time."

CHAPTER 3

A fter securing Timothy in his car seat, Elizabeth sat behind the steering wheel, hands in the ten o'clock and two o'clock position, clenching and unclenching her fists. Okay, breathe, she told herself. In through the nose and out through the mouth. Calming breaths. She glanced in the rearview mirror at her son. Timothy was content, playing with his fingers, two of which found their way into his mouth. Elizabeth grimaced. She always cleaned his hands immediately after leaving a doctor's office. You never know what germs were floating around such places and Timothy could not afford to get any sicker than he was. Upset at the possible negative prognosis Dr. Muller hinted at, she had completely forgotten about cleansers when she fled his office.

Why did she have to do this alone? Why couldn't Jackson have taken even just an hour off work to go with her? Part of her brain knew that he was already halfway across the State by now and had to travel for his job, but still…. This felt too much like single parenting, something she had not signed on for. She wasn't one of those strong, independent women; she needed a man to rely on. A man like her dad had been would be ideal. But those were rare commodities, and it wasn't fair to Jackson to compare him to her pretty much perfect dad. Well, he would still be perfect if he hadn't ended up dead, leaving her alone.

I'm not alone, she reminded herself. I have a beautiful son and a loving husband. We're fine.

~

E lizabeth uncrumpled the papers still locked between her fingers. She spread them out - yes, the prescriptions were still readable. And yes, she knew the routine of weaning Timothy off one medication, while gradually increasing the dose of a new one, recording side effects, and efficacies. She could do this. She had to.

~

S he made the drive to the pharmacy on autopilot. Great. Looked like Timothy was just falling asleep. He'd be cranky if she woke him. Sighing, she began loosening the straps on his car seat.

"Come on, big guy. We have to go see Mr. Rexton." A groggy Timothy leaned on his mom, the back of his head pressing into her neck. She hefted him up a little higher and with one arm firmly around his bottom, reached into the front seat for her purse, slinging it over her shoulder. Since she became a mother, there were no more clutch purses for her - only shoulder bags that would leave her hands free. This whole business was easier when Timothy was younger. Toting a forty-pound child was tougher than one might think. Who needed to go the gym when she did this all day?

~

Mr. Rexton's warm eyes greeted her. He always served Elizabeth himself rather than relying on his assistants. He took a special interest in Timothy. Elizabeth discovered that pharmacists held a wealth of knowledge and could help explain things she was too overwhelmed to ask her son's specialists, or didn't get the first time she heard them.

She handed over the new prescriptions. Sam Rexton raised his eyebrows. "Let's hope that these just might do the trick. How has the little tike been?"

"Obviously not well or well enough," Elizabeth replied, nodding at the prescriptions.

"Let me pull up his chart." After perusing the screen a minute, he asked, "Shall we go over the protocol for weaning him off of the valproic acid?" As they discussed the approach Dr. Muller laid out, Timothy stirred in her arms. It was one thing to hold a sleeping forty pounds, but another to keep a good grip on a squirming forty pounds. She slid him down her legs and steadied him until his feet seemed firmly planted, holding his right hand.

"We have a bit of a back-log right now, so it will take about twenty minutes for me to fill these. Do you want to wait?"

Timothy was pulling at her hand. "No, I think we'll come back. I have a bit of shopping to do then I'll fill the car with gas. We should be back within an hour or so."

The pharmacist pointed to the jar on the counter containing suckers. Elizabeth shook her head. "Still low carb so we're avoiding sweets. But thanks, anyway." Besides, such treats made such a sticky mess.

"See you soon," he told Timothy. "When you come back, I'll have a better treat waiting for you."

∾

S he didn't need much, just a few things at the grocery store. Some nuts, cheese and avocados. They didn't last well so she liked to buy them fresh a few times a week. While it had at first seemed daunting, the ketogenic diet wasn't that difficult to maintain once she had firmly in mind which foods to have on hand. The worst part was eliminating breads. Sandwiches were a quick meal for a child, but they'd learned to make do. Mostly, she and Jackson stuck to the diet as well, and they'd each lost a few extra pounds. While it had helped them, she was not so sure that the diet was having any effect on their son's seizures. But, as Dr. Muller said, maybe they'd be worse without this low-carb diet. She grabbed her insulated bag out of the trunk, and they went to pick up their groceries. This would be a fast trip because she had a surprise in mind for Jackson so would need to make time for an extra stop. No, it wasn't his birthday or their anniversary; she just wanted to do something nice and keep it in the freezer for when he got home Friday. She had placed an order for a Dairy Queen Ice Cream cake - his favorite Reeses-Pieces kind and would pick it up after she got groceries, then gas, then Timothy's prescriptions. And Jackson thought that all a housewife did was sit at home watching soaps.

~

J ackson liked to tease that she was such a creature of habit. Maybe that was true, but she found it easier to get chores done when she kept to a schedule. She filled the car with gas every Monday. When she first got her driver's license, her dad had drilled it into her to never let her gas tank get below half full because you just never knew. Only driving around town she used little gas, certainly not like poor Jackson who put thousands of miles on his car each month. The life of a traveling salesman. Elizabeth often wondered if Frankfurt Electric knew just what a gem of an employee they had in Jackson. She wasn't sure his take-home pay he showed her reflected his real worth. Despite the long hours he worked, they'd have a hard time living off just his wage. Good thing her father had the forethought to prepare a trust fund for her and bought their home as a wedding gift.

∼

Elizabeth pulled into the gas station, the same one she always went to. Sticking with the familiar made life easier - just one more thing that she didn't have to figure out during her day.

As she started the pump running, she watched her son's sleeping face through the side window. He looked so at peace. But she knew that even in his slumber a seizure could attack. Thankfully, there had been just one today.

When the nozzle clicked off, she placed it back on the pump, then shut her gas cap. She reached in the compartment in the driver's door for her hand sanitizer. You never knew who had last handled these gas pumps and what germs they might carry that she might pass on to Timothy. The seizures were far worse when he got sick.

After rubbing for the required thirty seconds, she replaced the sanitizer, grabbed her purse to head in to pay for her gas. Crossing the pavement, she felt the sun on her hair and wiped her forehead with the back of her arm.

She hated perspiring; it was not her thing. Goodness, it was a blistering afternoon.

Hot. She glanced back at her slumbering son. The temperature inside a closed car could rise quickly, and Timothy had already been in the car almost five minutes while she pumped the gas. Getting overheated was one condition that brought on seizures. Should she wake him up and carry him inside with her? He was such a dead weight when he didn't want to awaken. She'd just be a few seconds inside and he would be in plain sight all the time.

Elizabeth returned to the car, slid in and started the engine, cranking up the air conditioning. It was the right thing to do; it was already uncomfortably hot inside. In the rear-view mirror, she could see that Timothy hadn't stirred. That neurologist appointment this morning must have taken as much out of him as it did out of her.

"Just a few more minutes, baby, then we'll head home and relax." Leaving the engine running, and leaving the door unlocked so she could get back in, Elizabeth went to pay for her gas.

She timed it poorly, and there were two people ahead of her in line. But then it was finally her turn. "I'm on pump five, please." She placed her purse on the counter to rummage through to find her wallet. Her purse was cavernous. Who would have known you had to carry around so much stuff for one small child?

The gas station attendant repeated the price. "Yes, I just need to get my credit card," Elizabeth mumbled, face pointed into the cavern of her shoulder bag. Opening her wallet, the first thing she saw was the picture of her son, taken on his fourth birthday. It always warmed her heart, that picture. Timothy with his arms around his parents, all wearing silly party hats.

Pulling the wallet out, she glanced at the car where Timothy sat, oblivious to the world.

She froze like a mannequin posed in a catatonic position. She could not take in what her eyes were seeing.

What? Who was that? There was a man, and he was opening the driver's door. Wait! He was getting in. "Hey!"

Elizabeth took off, yelling. Whereas the gas station had been full when she pulled in, but now it was void of people - except for this strange man getting into her car.

The guy shut the door. She could see his hand go to the gear shift. He was going to take off!

She sprinted the last few steps, turning her ankle on the concrete lip, breaking off the heel of her shoe. The car crept forward. Her left hand grabbed for the rear door handle, latched on and pulled. The car was already moving and picking up speed. She threw herself inside, her torso sprawling atop Timothy's car seat, her legs dangling outside. As she attempted to right herself, her left shoe flew off as they bumped over the curb. She yanked her legs inside just as the car's momentum swung the door shut.

~

F ind *GONE* at https://books2read.com/ goneapsychologicalthriller/

MORE ABOUT THE AUTHOR

Dr. Sharon A. Mitchell lives on a farm, with her nearest neighbor several miles away. Does that seem like a setting to spark the imagination? It does for her.

She takes long walks with her hundred-pound German Shepherd dogs, Pickles and Dill. (She didn't name them - don't blame her).

Her current projects are writing more books in the series The Farmers of Goodrich County - clean and wholesome romances with down-to-earth heroes, and heroines who are more than their match.

She's also working on her eighth psychological thriller novel for the *When Bad Things Happen* series.

In addition to short stories tied to that series, she's written six other novels, each featuring an autistic child or young adult. Two nonfiction books accompany that autism series.

Sharon's been a teacher, counselor, psychologist and consultant for decades and continues to teach university classes on kids who learn differently to soon-to-be teachers and administrators.

She loves to hear from her readers and always responds. Email her at sharon@sharonmitchellauthor.com.

Follow her to be notified of her next books on any of these social media links:

bookbub.com/authors/sharon-a-mitchell

facebook.com/DrSharonAMitchell

twitter.com/AutismSite

instagram.com/autismsite

pinterest.com/mitchellsha3047

ALSO BY DR. SHARON A. MITCHELL

Autism Novels and Nonfiction

Autism Goes to School

Autism Runs Away

Autism Belongs

Autism Talks and Talks

Autism Grows Up

Autism Goes to College

Autism Box Set

Autism Questions Parents Ask & the Answers They Seek

Autism Questions Teachers Ask & the Answers They Seek

www.ingramcontent.com/pod-product-compliance
Lightning Source LLC
Chambersburg PA
CBHW032040090426
42744CB00004B/69